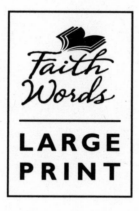

Good Health, Good Life

12 Keys to Enjoying Physical and Spiritual Wellness

JOYCE MEYER

LARGE PRINT

Copyright © 2014 by Joyce Meyer

Unless otherwise noted, all Scripture quotations are from *The Amplified Bible*. Copyright © 1954, 1958, 1962, 1964, 1965, 1987 by The Lockman Foundation. Used by permission.

Scripture quotations marked NKJV are from the New King James Version. Copyright © 1979, 1980, 1982 by Thomas Nelson, Inc. Used by permission. All rights reserved.

Scripture quotations marked NIV are from the HOLY BIBLE, NEW INTERNATIONAL VERSION. Copyright © 1973, 1978, 1984 International Bible Society. Used by permission of Zondervan Bible Publishers.

FaithWords
Hachette Book Group
1290 Avenue of the Americas
New York, NY 10104

www.faithwords.com

Printed in the United States of America

RRD-C

First Edition: December 2014

10 9 8 7 6 5 4 3 2 1

FaithWords is a division of Hachette Book Group, Inc.
The FaithWords name and logo are trademarks of Hachette Book Group, Inc.

The Hachette Speakers Bureau provides a wide range of authors for speaking events. To find out more, go to www.hachettespeakersbureau.com or call (866) 376-6591.

The publisher is not responsible for websites (or their content) that are not owned by the publisher.

Library of Congress Cataloging-in-Publication Data has been applied for.

ISBN 978-1-4555-4714-2 (hardcover)—ISBN 978-1-4555-3021-2 (large print)

CONTENTS

INTRODUCTION

Do you have any idea how valuable you are? You are so valuable that God gave His only Son not only to forgive your sins and to give you eternal life, but also so you can enjoy abundant life—life to the fullest—while you are on this earth. I believe God has a great life in store for you. He wants you to enjoy every single day of it and to serve Him to the best of your ability for as long as you live. Doing these things can be very difficult if you do not feel well, if you live under constant stress, or if you are not in good health. But if you are strong and healthy, then making the most of every day God gives you is much easier.

Good health is vitally important to being able to live a good life. God's plan for our lives involves much more than simply praying and reading the Bible every day, going to church or doing missions work. He cares about every part of us and about every aspect of our lives. He wants us to be healthy not only spiritually, but also physically, mentally, and emotionally. That's the best way for us to enjoy our lives and fulfill all the purposes God has for us.

We know from 1 Corinthians 6:19-20 that our bodies are the earthly temples of the Holy Spirit. In other words, our bodies are our God-given instruments for experiencing life on Earth and for serving God and blessing other people. They house our spirit, which is the part of our being where God dwells. God Himself lives in us by His Spirit and makes His home in us. That is the best reason I know for us to take care of ourselves.

Sometimes, over the years, we neglect our health or let our bodies go for various reasons. Often, we simply get busy and stressed, and we think we do not have time to take care of ourselves. The fact is, people who do not believe they have time to take care of themselves when their health is relatively good will more than likely experience health problems and/or a lack of energy eventually. If you form a habit of taking care of yourself, doing so will simply become a part of your lifestyle and you won't find it difficult. In fact, you will enjoy investing in your health.

We also need to realize that we are more than just physical beings. We are three-part beings—spirit, soul (mind, will, and emotions), and body—and each one needs proper care and maintenance (1 Thessalonians 5:23). If we do not take good care of our bodies, our spiritual, mental, and emotional health will be compromised. If we worry excessively, that can have a negative impact on our bodies. If we have a lot of emotional trauma, it adds stress that affects us physically. If we don't invest in our spiritual life, it will grow weak and nothing will work right for us. To be healthy and whole, we need to be strong in spirit, soul, and body.

I take very good care of myself now in every way, but that has not always been the case. The lessons I will share with you in this book are lessons I learned firsthand on my journey out of bad health habits into good ones. As I moved from being an unhealthy person to being a strong, healthy individual, I had to learn about healthy eating, exercise, proper rest, managing stress effectively, and many other aspects of good health and a good life.

I want to encourage you: Whatever shape you are in today, you do not have to stay that way. If you want to improve the way you look and feel, you can do that by reading this book and applying its insights and information to your life. If your "temple" (body) is in need of some restoration or renovation, you have chosen a resource that can help. Your entire being—spirit, soul, and body—plays an important role in God's plan, and the healthier you are in all three ways, the better your life will be.

I am believing that the 12 keys in this book will unlock a whole new level of health and well-being for you, empowering you to do everything God has called you to do and to enjoy the great future He has in store for you.

HOW TO USE THE 12-KEY PLAN FOR GOOD HEALTH

Maybe you have heard the saying, "Rome wasn't built in a day." That phrase simply means nothing truly great happens overnight. The best things in life take time to grow, to develop, and to become established. Your personal health is one of these things. It's an ongoing project, something you will need to be attentive to for the rest of your life. But like any big project, you begin with a solid foundation and build from there. That's what this book is all about. Each of the following 12 chapters, called "keys," explains one important element of building a lifestyle that nurtures a healthy, sound body, soul, and spirit. Your task is to read each key and decide if you need to improve that area of your life. If so, the book will help you figure out how to do it.

In each key, I will explain what the important principle is and why it is vital to physical and spiritual health. Then, I'll make several suggestions for incorporating that change into your life. At the end of each key, I will ask you to choose to take as many of those suggestions as you feel you need and write them in the space provided. You may end up doing all of them, or you may end up doing only one or two. The important thing is to do whatever you need most. There's no need to be in a hurry about them. Just work on one at a time, without trying to tackle them all at once, and over a period of time you'll see great improvements in your health and well-being. In the back of this book, I have provided a place for you to jot down the changes you commit to in each key, so at the end of the book you will have a list of the lifestyle changes you have adopted. If you really incorporate these changes into the way you live, you will be amazed at the positive changes they will bring to your life.

If you are wondering how long you will need to spend on each key, that's entirely up to you. The important thing to do is to put in enough effort that each one gets established and becomes a new habit for you. Certainly, taking a new key every day would be too fast, but taking a new key each month would not necessarily be too slow. It would simply mean you would spend the next year committing yourself to a firm foundation of physical and spiritual health; in addition, it would give you plenty of time to work on each key before moving on to the next. You might even want to begin this process by reading the entire book quickly so you can have an idea of what you are working toward, then go back and take each key one at a time, putting into each one the kind of effort that is right for you before moving to the next. The pace at which you will need to work through this book depends on how quickly you adapt to change and how eager you are to develop a healthier way of life. I would prefer you take more time and achieve lasting success than rush through the book and not be able to sustain any of the changes it can bring to your life.

You certainly don't have to do the keys in

the order in which they appear in the book, but it would be a good idea because each one builds on the one that precedes it. The first few keys (dealing with right relationship with God, good self-esteem and healthy body image, and strong metabolism) provide a solid foundation for the rest.

As I mentioned earlier, I do recommend reading the entire book before going back and focusing on each key in a diligent and committed way. Think about the big-picture goals you have for your future health and well-being, then let each key serve as a small step toward that larger vision. Keep those long-term goals in sight and determine to reach them one step at a time.

Got it? Now let's get going! It's time to take your first step toward a new you!

Good Health, Good Life

KEY
1

Get God's Help

Most of us want to look great and feel great. We want to be in good health and to enjoy our lives. That is certainly true for me, as I am sure it is for you, but for years I did not go about it the right way. If you can name a diet invented in the past 40 years, chances are I have tried it. I have attempted to lose weight with low-fat diets, low-carb diets, liquid diets, hard-boiled egg diets, and the grapefruit diet. Some of those eating plans even worked—at first. But you may know what happens with a lot of fad diets: A person is excited to get started because of the promise of success, but after a while, even if weight loss happens, the diet becomes inconvenient, boring, or extremely difficult to sustain long term. When people reach this point, they often begin to stray from the diet. They only cheat a little bit at first, but eventually they revert to their old, familiar eating habits and regain the weight they lost. Sometimes they end up weighing even more than they did when they started dieting, wishing they had never tried to lose weight in the first place.

I have been through this scenario countless times. Maybe you have too. When it happens, we feel guilty. We think we are to blame for our failure. If we only had more willpower when we found a diet that "worked," we reason, we would still be on it and we would still be losing weight and looking great. We criticize ourselves for lack of willpower, but maybe what's actually happening is that we do not fully understand the principle of willpower. What if we are leaving something out? What if there is something we are not aware of, but must understand, in order for willpower to work? Maybe we just need to know the truth about willpower.

God's Power Is Better Than Willpower

Willpower sounds like a great thing. We have been trained to believe that if we have enough of it, we can fight off every temptation that comes our way. Sometimes, that is true. But let me tell you a little secret about willpower: Willpower is your best friend when things are going well, but when you begin to get weary or stressed, it runs out on you. Willpower looks out the window on a morning you have promised yourself you will go for a jog, and says, "Oh, it's raining and it's forty degrees and I'm so warm and toasty in bed. I am going to stay home and read today."

The problem with willpower is that it is closely related to reasoning. And reason is *always* open to being "reasoned" with and talked out of things. Reason says to willpower, "You're right. It's way too cold and messy for you to go jogging today. You can run twice as far tomorrow." Or, "Go ahead and eat that extra piece of pie. That way you can put the pie plate in the dishwasher. You can just eat a really small dinner tonight." It makes sense! But we must know that reason is always willing to take the first step down the slippery slope that leads to failure.

I have found that if I really do not want to do something, my mind gives me plenty of reasons not to do it. My emotions even join in, saying, "You really don't feel like doing that anyway." Our souls (remember, the soul comprises the mind, will, and emotions) would love to run our lives, but the Bible says we are to be led by God's Spirit, not by the human soul. In other words, we are not to be willpower-led; we are to be Spirit-led. God says in Zechariah 4:6, "Not by might nor by power, but by My Spirit" (NKJV). This means we can have plenty of willpower and discipline, but those alone are not always enough. Doing things by the Spirit of God and relying on His power are the only ways to find true success. Willpower and determination may get us started on the right path to some worthy goal, but they have a reputation for quitting in the middle. The Spirit of God never quits in the middle; He always gets us all the way across the finish line to the victory He wants us to enjoy. By all means use discipline, self-control, and willpower, but first and foremost depend on God's power to energize you in all of these areas.

Some people claim to be a "self-made success," but if we study their lives and follow them through to the end, we see that these people often end up falling apart. This is because they tried to do everything themselves. God has not created us to function well without Him. In fact, Jesus says in John 15:5: "Apart from Me [cut off from vital union with Me] you can do nothing." The sooner we learn this lesson and invite God to do the heavy lifting in our lives, the better off we will be.

Breaking Bondages

Whether a person's weakness is overeating, some type of substance addiction, or simply a pattern of poor personal maintenance, he or she is in bondage and unable to lead the life God intends until these things are broken and dealt with. God has an awesome plan for all of us, but it requires us to understand and exercise the amazing power we have as His children. In Him, everyone can break free from old destructive habits and start living the new and exciting life of freedom God has for us, but we need His help.

Freedom is our natural desire. It is also the condition God wants and has provided for us, but if we have fallen into bondage over time, the thought of freedom can be scary. We may prefer the comfort and ease of our familiar bonds to making the effort needed to develop the thoughts and behaviors required for freedom. This is sad, but some people really would rather endure poor diets, low energy, compromised health, self-neglect, and exhaustion than do what is necessary to taste freedom and develop a lifestyle of liberty. This is because these people find change extremely challenging and difficult.

I have found that the only thing more frightening than change is the thought of never changing. Genuine, permanent change about why we are not caring for ourselves may require some deep soul-searching, and not everyone is willing to do that. Only the truth sets us free (John 8:32), but truth is not always easy to face. In fact, facing the truth about ourselves and about our habits is one of the bravest things we can do, and it is the key to being set free to live a better life. This is what God wants for us, and He will help us in every way.

Let God Bear the Burden

Sometimes the journey toward long-term good health can seem unbearable. When you are discouraged about the condition of your life or the shape your body is in, the first step toward improvement seems like the most difficult one in the world. A short-term crash diet may appear to be easier than a lifetime of steady movement toward great health, but it will not bring freedom. Temporary relief never equals true freedom. God wants you to be free!

Soul-searching, facing truth, and making necessary changes will indeed be unbearable if you try to bear them alone. The bonds of old habits are too strong and the forces against you are too formidable. Only God is strong enough to accomplish what needs to be done in your life. If you will turn things over to Him, the source of divine strength and enablement, you will find the power you need to break free. If you will draw on the limitless power of the Holy Spirit, rather than relying on your own limited abilities, He will always lead you to victory and freedom.

As you begin your journey toward greater and greater health, I hope you will memorize this verse and gain strength from it: "But those who wait on the Lord shall renew their strength; they shall mount up with wings like eagles, they shall run and not be weary, they shall walk and not faint" (Isaiah 40:31, NKJV). God is ready and eager to help you become a stronger, healthier person. Let Him do the heavy lifting for you!

Five Ways to Let God Help

1. Ask

You will be amazed at what a huge difference it makes to directly invite God into your life to help solve your problems. Take time to quiet your mind and open it to Him. Then ask Him to be your partner on the journey to personal restoration and holistic health. Ask Him specifically to help you make wise choices and give you the discipline you need to enjoy good health and a good life, for the rest of your life.

2. Attend Church

Studies have shown that people of faith, people who are involved in church, and people who practice prayer and Bible study live longer and are generally healthier than people who do not go to church or live lives of faith. Some people manage to maintain good relationships with God for many years without much support from others, but they are few and far between. Most of us find that a weekly boost of Christian teaching and a community of fellow believers provide a much stronger bond with God than we could maintain on our own. If you are struggling to make contact with God or to grow spiritually and you have not tried church, what are you waiting for? It could improve your life drastically!

3. Participate in a Support Group

Support groups exist for a variety of issues, from alcohol or drug addiction to grief to overeating. They can help you acknowledge that you really cannot break your bondage by yourself and encourage you to turn over your restoration to God. Many people can make better progress and stay more committed to their goals for health and well-being if they have the support of other individuals who are going through the same process. If you are a person who succeeds best when others are on a journey with you, try finding a support group and then maximize the benefits of it. If being in a group is not desirable to you, then perhaps you can find one person to be accountable to, someone you can share with and depend on to pray for you.

4. **Begin Each Day with an Affirmation**
When you first wake up in the morning, before the busy-ness of the day begins, take a moment to renew your commitment to God and refresh yourself with reminders of the truth of His Word. This will give you the mental and emotional peace that is the foundation for success. You can also write and declare an affirmation that addresses your specific needs or you can use this one that I wrote:

"God, I am free by the power of Your Word. I believe You have given me the strength to break free from the bonds that have been holding me back from all the good things You have planned for me. I thank You that I am free by the blood of Jesus and the sacrifice He made on the cross of Calvary. Thank You for making me free through the truth of Your Word and for empowering me with Your strength and wisdom. Help me to be all You want me to be. In Jesus' name, amen."

5. Deal with Your Doubts and Struggles Through Prayer

No matter who you are, you will have moments when your determination weakens, when you are sorely tempted not to do what you have committed to do as a key to lifetime health. When you feel that way, don't quit, but do not struggle trying to do it on your own either. Instead, acknowledge your struggle, step back, and take a moment to ask God to help you do what you need to do. Let Him renew your strength in that moment of peace, then move forward with new passion, trust, and confidence.

Act on It

Which of the five actions in this key will you take so you can walk more closely with God and let Him help you on your journey toward greater and greater health? Write them below, commit to them, and start today.

Deal with my doubts Struggles Through Prayer

Begins each day with Affirmation

Let God bear the burden By calling Him in to Your Solution

KEY
2

Learn to Love Your Body

What if, everywhere you went, you ran into someone you did not like? Wouldn't that be terrible? *Oh no,* you would think, *it's* her *again.* If you went to a party, you would have to endure her conversation. If you went to church, she would sit right beside you. You would never enjoy going anywhere because everywhere you went, there she was. But it gets even worse. What if she went home with you? What if she sat at your table for every meal and even showed up in your bedroom?

The situation I have described sounds awful, but it is the situation you are in if you do not like yourself, because you are everywhere you go. You cannot get away from yourself, even for a second. People who dread their own company are in for a sad life.

The troubles that could arise from not liking yourself may seem obvious, but believe it or not, I have found that a lot of people do not like themselves. They may not even be aware of it, but some genuine soul-searching reveals the fact that they have a habit of rejecting themselves and in some cases they even hate themselves. I have come across a lot of people over the years in my ministry and in day-to-day life, and I am amazed at how few are truly at peace with who they are. Instead, they have declared war on themselves, frequently because of the way they feel about their bodies.

Why People Despise or Reject Their Bodies

How can so many of us hate our bodies, our faithful servants that exist to help us become all God wants us to be while we are here on Earth? I can think of several reasons.

1. Abuse During Childhood

We are all born with loving attitudes toward our bodies. Small children instinctively enjoy their bodies; they care for and protect them. They never think about what their bodies look like until they are older. But this natural understanding of the goodness of their bodies changes when someone mistreats them, mishandles them, or sends them negative messages about the way they look. I know this firsthand. The physical and emotional abuse I suffered as a child told me loud and clear that my body was bad and I was worthless.

I know from experience that when pain and discomfort are the only physical experiences people have, they learn to hate their bodies as the sources of those feelings. Sometimes they even want to punish their bodies for the bad things "they" did to them. Even when these people become adults, their disrespect and disgust for their bodies remain, even if the abuse stops. And when people do not live in harmony with their bodies, all sorts of bad situations develop. They do not exercise or eat healthily because they do not want to care for or treat well something that has caused so much pain and trauma.

Abuse does not have to be physical or sexual to cause problems. Authority figures or even peers are perfectly capable of driving home messages that we are bad or useless and our bodies are ugly and evil. If you have been abused, as I was, please know that until you confront your feelings and find peace, you will be constantly at war with yourself and will experience the stress, trauma, and exhaustion that war causes. God wants you to be healthy and at peace, and so do I.

People who have roots of shame about who they are will be poisoned from the inside out. Those poisoned roots must be replaced with God's unconditional love and acceptance. We must learn to love ourselves—including our bodies—in balanced ways and embrace who we are at this moment in time. I believe that if we love and respect our bodies more, they will serve us better.

2. Misunderstanding the Bible's Teachings

The Bible tells us to resist the flesh and submit to the spirit, but that does not mean we are to hate our fleshly bodies. The flesh is weak and the spirit is strong, so we need to use the spirit's strength to lovingly guide the flesh.

The human body is the temple of the Holy Spirit. People around me cannot see my spirit. All they can see is my body, so if I am going to spread God's love, I have to use my body to do it! My hands need to be the hands of Jesus; my feet, His feet; and my mouth, His mouth.

Romans 12:1 teaches us to offer all of our faculties as a living sacrifice for

God's use. Learn to love your body as a means of giving glory to God.

3. Media Messages

The media use all kinds of tricks to make people look "perfect." Lighting, photo editing, and airbrushing can work wonders on a movie star or a magazine cover model, but who in the real world has access to those things? No one I know can slim her thighs with a computer cursor before she goes out each day!

I don't think the media are trying to make us feel unattractive or bad about ourselves. I think they simply know people are drawn to beauty, so they try to sell us their products by showing as much beauty as possible, even if it is altered or fake.

What really makes us feel inferior to models and movie stars is our ego, the part of our psyche that finds meaning by figuring out how we compare with other people. The problem with ego is that there is always someone prettier, smarter, or richer than we are. Ego can always find something to feel bad about; it is never satisfied and it continually pushes us to compete with others.

I stopped competing a long time ago. I am at peace with my body. I love and support it, and it supports me. I do not feel any need to look like a model. I simply expect my body to reflect who I am—a healthy, happy woman who wants to serve God in every way I can. I try to look my best, but I do not allow myself to be pressured by unrealistic expectations the media creates and I hope you won't either.

4. The Beauty Industry

For people who do not like themselves, the beauty industry can be even more dangerous than the media. The media can make us feel bad about ourselves by showing us extraordinarily beautiful people, but the beauty industry tries to make us feel we will never look the way

we "should" without their products.
The truth is, we are already beautiful
in God's eyes and if we accept ourselves
and follow His principles, we will have
inner beauty and we will look better
and better on the outside too.

God loves you. He wants you to
receive His love and accept yourself.
I encourage you to receive His love
today and begin to take care of yourself
because you realize how much He cares
for you and how valuable you are to
Him. When you have a good relationship with God and know your value,
you will not be desperate for the newest
skin cream, makeup product, or beau-
tification program.

5. Age and Sickness

You can grow up in a loving and supportive environment, be comfortable
with your looks, and be immune to the
spells of the media and the beauty industry, but still fall out of love with your
body as you age. As years go by, your

activity level decreases, your metabolism slows, you may gain a few pounds, your joints may not feel quite as limber as they once did, and suddenly everyone around seems thinner, faster, and younger than you. If you have experienced certain illnesses, they may also leave you weakened in some way or cause you to be frustrated with your body.

Whatever your situation is, be content. As the saying goes, "It is what it is," so make the best of it. Do what you can do, and don't be bitter and frustrated about what you cannot do. Even if your capacity to exercise is limited, be diligent to do everything you can still do. I recently had a stress fracture in one of my toes, and although I could not do some of the exercises I normally do, I continued to do what I could do. Another time I had an injured shoulder that took several months to heal, but I kept doing the exercises I could do while being careful not to re-injure the shoulder.

Throughout your life, continue to eat right, drink plenty of water, and get good sleep. Above all, regardless of your age or medical condition, keep a positive attitude because that will have a positive impact on your health.

Five Ways to Nurture Self-Love

1. Don't Chase Your Youth

Although I am 70 years old I feel really great—which shows that things like energy, health, and happiness do not have to decline as we grow older. But part of my health comes from the contentment of being comfortable with who I am. I have succeeded at being myself. I do not pine away for my 20s, partly because I did not like my 20s anyway, and partly because it would not matter if I did. Here I am now, and I have chosen to live today!

People who long for their youth are never content, because every day a little more of that youth slips away. Aging is a fact of life and we need to learn to do it gracefully while remaining young at heart. Discontent is one of the biggest giants we must conquer if we ever hope to enjoy life fully. Being dissatisfied with our looks, age, position in life, possessions, or anything else makes us ungrateful for what we currently have. We may not have everything we want, but we certainly have more than some people.

I encourage you to embrace aging with a healthy attitude. Don't despise the aging process, because if you stay alive you cannot avoid it. Cheer up and make the best of things. Love yourself and love your life; it's the only one you have!

2. Learn to Receive God's Love

The greatest gift that can ever be given is offered to each of us every day, yet few of us have the faith and self-esteem needed to truly accept and embrace it. God offers us His love. All we have to do is open our hearts and make the decision to receive it. Receiving God's love is an important step because we cannot love others if we have not accepted His love for us. We cannot give away what we do not have.

Receiving is an action. It involves a conscious decision to reach out and take hold of something. Think of a wide receiver in a football game. He is not called the "wide target." He does not just stand in one place and wait for the quarterback to put the ball in his hands. No, he wants that football and he goes after it aggressively.

This is how we need to think about receiving God's love. We need to be hungry for it and passionate about it. I encourage you to go after it, study it, and meditate on it. As you seek it eagerly, you will receive a life-changing revelation of God's love deep in your heart.

3. Focus on the Journey, Not the Destination

I remember as a child feeling that it took forever to get anywhere when my family traveled by car. I was so excited about our destination that the hours of driving were like torture! As an adult, I spent a lot of miserable years never enjoying where I was because I was too focused on where I wanted to go. I finally learned that life is about the journey, not the destination, and the ride has become a lot more fun.

On your personal journey toward good health and a good life, I hope you will also enjoy the ride. What matters most is not where you are right now or how far away your destination is, but the direction in which you are headed. Don't ever be discouraged that you have not reached your destination. Be excited that you are heading in the right direction. Where your health is concerned, the important thing is not what you weigh today, how flexible your joints

are, or how far you can run, but that
you are improving. Keep a positive attitude about your progress, and that will
breed more progress.

Jesus says, "Do not worry or be anx-
ious about tomorrow, for tomorrow will
have worries and anxieties of its own"
(Matthew 6:34). In other words, focus
on today. Be proud of what you can do
today. Don't go beyond that. Instead of
looking at how far you have to go, look
at how far you have come. Fill each
day with fellowship with God, good
choices, healthy foods, lots of activity,
and positive thoughts. Then your body
and soul will be healthy, fit, and virtu-
ous. As you learn to enjoy the journey,
you will discover how easy it is to love
and affirm yourself.

4. Focus on Health, Not Pounds

In the United States, we seem to be
obsessed with weight, but the truth is that
fitness should be much more important
to us than pounds. We need to be more

health-conscious than weight-conscious. I firmly believe that if we concentrate on good health, we will weigh what we are supposed to weigh.

We live in an age when "thin is in," and our attitudes toward fat run close to hysteria. Lose weight if you feel you need to, but do not let anyone tell you that your weight is unhealthy or unnatural if it isn't. And by all means, don't let a few pounds keep you from loving and accepting yourself or from pursuing good general, overall health. Learning to major on your health and minor on your weight may be a whole new way of thinking for you, but I believe it is vital to your health. I firmly believe that if you focus on eating right and being healthy, you will ultimately weigh what is right for you.

5. View Your Body as Your Friend

If your body is larger than you would like, with aches and pains you are tired of, don't treat it as an enemy. If you do, you may never see progress in the areas you would like to improve. If you had a friend who was sick or in need, you would do everything you could do to help that person. This is exactly the attitude you should have toward your body. If it is not what you want it to be, do all you can to help it; don't despise it or reject it.

We blame our bodies for a lot of things they are not responsible for. After all, our bodies are the products of what we have put into them and the ways we have treated them for years and years. I would not blame my car for falling apart if I put glue in the gas tank instead of fuel. Whatever problems we have, the fault lies with us, not with our bodies. We may have made poor choices, but the good news is that we can begin to reverse them.

Accept your body today as your friend and companion for life. Start taking care of it as you would care for your best friend and develop a great relationship with it, one that will keep you strong and healthy for years to come.

Act on It

Which of the five actions in this key will you take so you can learn to love your body and take better care of it as you move toward greater health? Write them below, commit to them, and start today.

_____

_____

_____

KEY
3

Master Your Metabolism

Have you ever wished you could own a masterpiece, like an original van Gogh or a Monet? You may think you could never afford such a masterwork, but the truth is, you were born with one. The human body is God's own masterpiece. Part of what makes it so special is its amazing versatility. You were made to survive in all kinds of situations, which is why your body is so adaptable. If you soak up a lot of sun, your body automatically produces extra pigment in your skin to protect you. If you use your muscles every day, your body starts making those muscles bigger to help you out. What a system!

One way the body constantly adapts is

through its metabolism. We hear and use this term often. For example, if we see a woman who is thin and highly energetic, or a man who eats huge amounts of food but never gains weight, we say that person has a high metabolism. People who are less energetic and gain weight easily often say they have a slow metabolism. But what do we really mean by *metabolism?* And what impact does it have on our weights, our waistlines, and our energy levels?

The Power System for Your Body

Metabolism is simply the process by which your body breaks down, or metabolizes, your food and converts it into energy. All your energy comes from the food you eat (despite what certain pills or supplements may claim); it's like fuel for your body. You literally burn that food, which powers your body and your brain just as your car burns gasoline to power its movement.

When your metabolism feels sluggish, it means you are creeping along like a car stuck in first gear. You are not burning much food, which means you do not have much energy. You feel down and uninspired, lethargic and slower than the people around you. That's not a good situation for your body or for your brain.

If your body is not using much energy but you are still filling your "tank" with as much food as usual, you will soon be in trouble. Think of it this way: If you put more gas in your car than you can use, the extra liquid spills out the top of the tank and runs down the side of your car, wasted. But your body is more sophisticated than your car. It has an incredibly flexible system for storing excess. It will store as much as you give it. Millions of special, pliable cells throughout your body swell up with the extra fuel, saving it for later. They are called fat cells.

The body has another survival trick. Not only does it store energy for the future in the form of fat, it also tries to be careful about the rate at which it uses these fat resources. You may run your household in a similar way. If you get a promotion at work and your income increases, you loosen your purse strings a bit. Maybe you redecorate, build an addition, put in a swimming pool, or start taking nicer vacations. On the other hand, if you lose your job or have a reduction in your pay, you immediately cut back on expenses to try to get by as long as possible on your savings. You hold off on new purchases, turn down the heat during the winter, and travel less.

Your body works the same way. If it does not get much food (or water), it assumes hard times are here and does what it can to get you through. It says, "Whoa, let's slow things down until some good food comes along." Figuratively speaking, it turns off the lights, turns down the heat, and tries to travel as little as possible. In other words, it slows down your metabolism. And you know what that feels like. You don't want to move. Your brain is groggy. You feel cold. You do not do much of anything. You just feel down. And you are burning very few calories, which will not help at all if you are trying to lose weight.

Why Diets Backfire

I hope you are beginning to see that unhealthy diets wreck metabolism. Any diet that tries to achieve weight loss by drastically cutting back on the number of calories you eat is doomed because it is based on a misunderstanding of how the human body works. It seems logical enough: Eat less, burn more, lose weight. And yes, that is the path to weight loss. The only way to lose weight is to burn more calories per day than you consume. When that happens, the body liquidates your fat reserves and burns them to make up the extra calories. You literally melt that fat right off of your body!

But as I just explained, your body's natural instinct is not to keep reviving your metabolism once your food intake goes way down. Not long after you start dieting, it will lower your metabolism to match the new amount of food it receives. This explains the classic dieting dilemma: You go on a diet and have great success the first few weeks. The pounds fall off and you think you've got it made. But then, even though you are sticking to the diet, even if it is difficult, suddenly the weight loss stops. You lose a couple of pounds one week, then one the next week, then none.

As this is happening, you can also feel sluggish and depressed, and you may crave "real" food. Soon you start sneaking forbidden foods and slipping off the diet. Then the weight comes back with a vengeance!

This happens because your body is happy to add an extra pound of fat but reluctant to give one up. Pounds go on easier than they come off. When your metabolism is slow and you are not doing much, you tend to lose muscle. The more you work a muscle, the bigger it gets, and the less you use it, the more it shrinks. Muscle looks great; it stays firm and flexes when you move, as opposed to fat, which has no shape and simply jiggles. More important, muscle burns calories all the time, just keeping itself ready for action. The more muscle you have, the more calories you burn, even when sleeping. This is called your *resting metabolism,* and it's different for every person.

Eventually, if you keep eating healthy foods regularly, your body catches up and starts increasing your metabolism. Most health experts recommend eating six small meals per day or forming the habit of eating something every two and a half to three hours. The six meals should be three meals and three snacks. Believe it or not this keeps the metabolism working and your body begins to burn calories at a faster rate. Keep in mind that the meals need to be healthy foods. Lots of vegetables and good protein as well as good fat can be a guideline. Fruit is also good, but lean toward more vegetables than fruit.

Dieting excessively and not taking in enough fuel may cause you to lose fat, but it also causes loss of muscle. You could even weigh the same as you did before dieting because muscle weighs more than fat, but you will look worse—because you have replaced firm muscle with fat—and you will burn fewer calories each day because you have less muscle and a lower resting metabolism. So you will find it more difficult than ever to maintain your weight. For all these reasons, dieting is not the way to reach or maintain a healthy weight.

The good news is that you can do plenty of things to fix this situation. The key is to eat a normal, balanced diet and to engage in activities that keep your metabolism purring along at an energetic clip. Do this and you will gradually shed excess pounds until you reach a healthy weight. Remember, the goal is not just to be thin, but to be healthy and weigh what is right for you. When we lose weight properly it will take longer, but the weight is more likely to stay off than if we lose it quickly on an unhealthy or fad diet of some kind.

Five Ways to Boost Metabolism

1. Exercise

The most popular and most effective way to burn calories is to move. Your body assumes that if you move fast every day, you have a good reason; it must be key to your survival. So it raises metabolism, builds more muscle, and gives you the enzymes you need to burn calories more easily. The more regularly you exercise, the higher you keep your metabolism and the more effortlessly those pounds will melt away. A fringe benefit of this is that you stay alert and happy more of the time.

2. Eat Breakfast (and Lunch and Dinner)

Most of us have heard that breakfast is the most important meal of the day, and that's true. Think about it: You fasted for hours while you slept. Your metabolism naturally slows down overnight, so breakfast is your body's signal to kick-start itself. A good breakfast gets all of your physical machinery working again—your digestion, brainpower, senses, muscles, and other systems. Because a good breakfast makes you so much more active, it can actually help you lose weight. Some people skip breakfast because they think that means they are eating less and therefore will lose weight. But failing to eat breakfast puts you in a state of lethargy; you creep through your morning, not accomplishing much of anything—including burning calories.

If you are a person who does not like the thought of eating anything in the morning or does not enjoy traditional breakfast foods, realize that breakfast does not have to be a big meal; even a little something will help get your metabolism going. But it cannot be just any "something." For example, eating sugary cereals is worse than eating nothing at all. Eating big loads of sugar or starch throws your system out of whack, makes you sleepy, and leads to numerous diseases. Make sure you get some protein at breakfast; try combining that with a little fat (which keeps you fuller longer) and with fruits or vegetables for vitamins and fiber. Here are some good breakfast choices:

- Eggs of any kind
- Yogurt, fruit, and nuts
- Peanut butter and whole-grain toast
- Lean meat (not fatty bacon or sausage)
- Whole-grain pancakes, waffles, or muffins
- Whole-grain cereal with fruit
- Whole-grain toast with cheese

Just as overlooking breakfast is not good for your health, skipping lunch or dinner is not a good idea either. Most people's bodies work best when they have regular amounts of food throughout the day. Generally speaking, we do not burn many calories after dinner, so a big dinner does little except convert to fat. Try eating a substantial breakfast and making dinner the lightest of the three meals of your day—and see how that improves your weight and your waistline.

3. Drink Water

I will address the importance of water in Key 6, but because it is so important to your metabolism, I want to make some basic observations about it here. Water is responsible for getting nutrients from your food to your muscles and your brain via blood, which is mostly composed of water. Your body uses water to do almost everything—to deliver nutrients to your cells, to cool yourself when you are hot, to flush waste, and to circulate immune cells through your body. Without enough water, all these systems start to suffer, and so does your metabolism. As you begin to dehydrate, you get sluggish because water is not there to transfer fuel to your muscles and brain. If you want to keep your metabolism at a high level, giving your body enough water every day is essential.

4. Sleep Well

Some people view sleep simply as "down time," but it is so much more than that.

Your conscious mind may be down, but lots of other parts of your body are hard at work performing vital maintenance tasks. As you sleep, your brain discharges the day's stress, your body repairs injuries, and your blood restocks your muscles with fuel for the coming day. Skip this vital part of a twenty-four-hour cycle and you will drag through the day with little energy, lowered metabolism, and poor performance on everything from tests or job reports to reaction time. In addition, lack of sleep will make you short tempered and cranky.

People tend to eat more when they are sleep deprived because they feel colder and less energetic, and they mistake these feelings for hunger. Get a decent night's rest and you will eat better, burn more calories overall, and have a better attitude and disposition.

5. Fidget

Research at the Mayo Clinic found that one major difference between overweight people and slender people may be how much they fidget. In other words, it isn't just planned exercise, such as workouts in the gym or walks in the park, but hundreds of tiny movements throughout the day that make the difference. The researchers found that all those little motions—getting up to look out a window, stretching, scratching your head, even shifting to the other side of the sofa to watch television—have a much bigger impact on health than anyone thought. People considered "skinny" fidgeted away 350 more calories a day than people who were overweight. That adds up to 35 pounds per year!

Starting today, take some steps to make your life a little bit more active by adding some intentional "fidgets."

- Take the stairs instead of the elevator.
- Walk as much as possible throughout your day. For example, don't

park close to the entrance of the place you are going. Park so you will have to walk a bit.

■ When you think of something you need to do, get up and do it. Don't procrastinate.

■ Choose activities that force you to move, such as gardening, dance classes, sweeping a porch or patio, or walking in the mall.

■ When you watch TV, get up and stretch periodically. Do the same at work.

■ Try putting your TV in front of a treadmill or exercise machine so you can exercise while you watch it.

■ Keep weights or exercise balls in your office and take a few minutes to use them throughout the day.

Act on It

Which of the five actions in this key will you take in order to master your metabolism as you move toward greater health? Write them below, commit to them, and start today.

_____

_____

_____

KEY
4

Exercise

Exercise works wonders to keep us healthy and strong. Sometimes, books and exercise programs give the impression that exercise is always fun and convenient. That certainly has not been my experience and maybe it has not been yours either. Whether you like it or not, exercising is an essential part of good health and a good life. It does so much to help us look great and feel great. There's simply no substitute for it.

Some people think they must go to a gym and work out with weights or expensive machines in order to exercise, but that is not true. There are many different ways to get exercise, including participating in active sports. Bike riding, running, and swimming are all great exercises. If you enjoy working out at a gym or having one in your home, go for it. But if you don't, then realize that gyms do not have a monopoly on exercise. There are many ways to get good exercise and most do not cost a lot of money, require special equipment, or cause you to have to rearrange your schedule. I know that if I am going to exercise every day, it must be something I can look forward to doing. I do work out at the gym and I have a trainer because I have found that works best for me. Knowing I have an appointment with someone three days a week helps me not to put it off until another time.

I also love walking in good weather. That not only gives me the cardiovascular workout essential for long life, it is also a great time to pray; it helps me feel more energetic throughout the day; and it does wonders for my stress level. In addition, I generally make sure I move a lot. I would not call myself "restless," but I do realize the importance of being mobile and I move around as often as possible. Regular exercise is a commitment and it takes time, but the benefits are well worth the effort. I began a regular exercise program seven years ago and have experienced tremendous benefits. I am smaller, and I have more energy, more stamina, and more muscle. I have even seen improvements in my skin tone. Exercise helps me mentally and it just feels good to know that I am investing in my health. Dave has been working out for more than 50 years. He is now 73 years old and looks absolutely amazing and has the energy of a much younger person.

I encourage you to begin now to incorporate exercise into your daily routine. The sooner you start, the sooner you can enjoy the positive changes exercise will bring to your health and to your life.

Stay Active

Once I started exercising, I quickly realized its benefits. I believe the same will be true for you. In addition to "traditional" exercise, you can also make an effort to keep your body active in as many small ways as possible. Remember that little things do add up! Just think about these things: If it's feasible, walk to a friend's house instead of driving. Use a push mower instead of a riding mower. If you work at a computer all day, get up and take regular breaks. If you want to go shopping, park at the opposite end of the mall from your favorite store and walk through the mall to get there.

I have handheld exercise balls on the couch in my office, and I also have a huge exercise ball nearby. Every so often I get up from my desk and bounce on the ball for five minutes. That gets my blood flowing, loosens my spine, and gives me a break from work, which is so important. I have found these balls to be very helpful and easy to use; you might want to try them too.

We need to make every effort to stay as active as we can. Short breaks and forced "inconveniences" in our days are necessary because we use our bodies so little these days. We have an abundance of appliances we can operate with only the push of a button. Very few of us have jobs that involve exercise and many of our leisure activities are spent with our feet up. This is a relatively new development in our culture and a dangerous one. Human beings were made to exercise. Our bodies are fit together with joints because God expects us to move a lot!

I admit, we do not read much in the Bible about Noah's workout routine or Moses' Pilates session. Does that mean people during Bible times did not get much exercise? Not at all! Everything they did involved exercise. Before automobiles, electricity, and machines, everything in the world ran on human power or animal power. If you wanted to get somewhere, you walked. If you needed to take something with you, you carried it. You did laundry by hand, chopped your own firewood, and milled your own grain. This physically active lifestyle may be one reason for the incredible longevity of biblical characters.

The best exerciser of all may have been Jesus. He routinely walked from His home in Galilee to Jerusalem—a distance of about

120 miles! Over the course of His ministry, He must have walked thousands of miles. In Jesus' day, people thought little of walking 10 miles to get somewhere. And because they walked such distances all their lives, their bodies were able to do that kind of exercise with ease. When I was in Moscow one time, I noticed that an unusually high number of the people I saw were slender. When I asked why, I was informed that most of them did not have cars and had to walk everywhere they went. So much daily walking definitely helps keep weight off and muscles strong.

Even as recently as the 1920s, people in American towns and cities walked an average of about two miles to work and school. Those walks alone burned around 200 calories per day, which is worth about 20 pounds a year in lost weight. When our society traded in daily walks for the convenience of automobiles, we did not realize we were setting ourselves up to gain 20 pounds in the process.

But weight loss is just the tip of the iceberg when it comes to the positive results of exercise. Yes, exercise will help you lose weight and look your best, but there are so many health benefits from regular exercise that go beyond the value of looks. Getting in shape for show is kind of like buying a new refrigerator because you like its color. That is a fine reason, but you may come to love its great new super-efficiency and extra-long warranty even more. And you can get those same things for your body through exercise. Other than not smoking, nothing can improve your health more.

Exercise is truly a "magic bullet." Just a few of the health conditions you can help prevent through exercise include arthritis, asthma, osteoporosis, stroke, Alzheimer's, depression, and gastrointestinal ills. If you exercise, you are also likely to get fewer colds, feel less stress, and better manage the stress you do feel. You will have less fat and more muscle, better tone and straighter posture, which means you will look great too.

Some common and serious diseases exercise may help you avoid include cardiovascular disease, diabetes, and cancer or other conditions affecting the immune system. Let me explain.

Heart Disease

Energy for exercise depends on getting enough oxygen and fuel to your muscles. Both of these things take place through an intricate process in the body and are accomplished through the bloodstream. Blood is your body's transportation network, and your heart drives it. As your demand for fuel and air increases, your heart pumps faster and faster, speeding the blood along on its important delivery route. The blood vessels that feed your exercising muscles dilate too, so they can carry more blood to the places that need it.

Regular exercise as simple as walking a couple of miles most days can cut your risk of heart disease and stroke in half! The best way to prevent these and other forms of cardiovascular disease is steady, moderate exercise, which keeps your blood vessels wide and clear and your heart strong.

Diabetes

The way the body breaks down sugar helps your muscles get the energy they need. Diabetes is a sugar disease caused by high levels of glucose (a type of sugar) in the blood. These high levels are the result of a diet high in fat, sugars, and starches, along with a sedentary lifestyle. You might think a lot of glucose would be a good thing—more energy—but elevated glucose levels over a long time cause lots of problems.

To understand this better, let me explain how glucose works in the body with insulin. Insulin is a hormone made by the pancreas and it acts like a key to "unlock" muscles so they will receive and absorb glucose. The more glucose people have in their blood, the more insulin they need. Eventually the muscles get stuffed and resist insulin's "unlocking" function. This is called "insulin resistance," and it sets in motion a process that ultimately results in diabetes.

A steady exercise program reduces your

chances of developing diabetes by nearly two-thirds. Combined with a healthy diet low in sugars, starches, and saturated fat, it makes your risk of diabetes negligible. For people who already have diabetes, no amount of exercise will reverse the disease, but it will help control glucose levels and allow these people to take as little insulin as possible.

Cancer and Immune Diseases

The connection between exercise and cancer prevention is not as direct as that between exercise and reduced cardiovascular disease or diabetes. Exercise has little impact on some cancers, yet it reduces the risk of breast cancer by 37% and provides similar protection against prostate and colon cancer. It does this by stimulating your immune system. Your immune defense, centered in the lymphatic system, circulates white blood cells through the body, where they find and eliminate cellular threats such as bacteria, viruses, and cancer cells. Unlike blood, which is pumped through the body by the heart, lymph depends on muscle contractions to squeeze it through the body. Moderate exercise more than doubles the rate at which your lymph circulates. The faster those white blood cells move, the more cancer cells and viruses they can pick off.

I hope you have learned in this key how much exercise can do to improve and preserve your health, and I hope you are ready to begin an exercise program you can stick with for years to come.

Five Ways to Start Exercising

1. **Take a Walk—Daily**

   Experts once thought people had to work up a good sweat in order to gain health benefits from exercise. They viewed walking as a fine way to take a break, but thought *real* exercise meant running, aerobic workouts, or other intense sports. As it turns out, that is not true. Researchers now know that most of the health benefits of exercise come from activities as simple as 30 minutes of walking every day. More intense exercise will burn more calories and cause a person to lose more weight, but will not increase longevity or do much to prevent disease.

Thirty minutes of walking means about two miles at a standard walking pace. It's not necessary to start out doing this much. If 15 minutes leaves you gasping, that is good enough as a starting place. Work your way up to 30 minutes at least five days a week. Eventually, two miles may seem too easy to you, so try pushing your distance up to three miles or do two miles at a faster pace. Keep yourself mildly challenged. Feel free to walk longer than 30 minutes if you can, though most people find that half an hour is all they can devote to exercise on a busy day. If you would like to use a book for guidance, try Dr. Don Colbert's *Walking in Divine Health*.

2. Exercise Indoors

I'm an outdoor walker. I love the chance to experience the day and the changing seasons from a path or a fairway. Thankfully, I live in a place where I can do this. But some people find it too hard to maintain an outdoor exercise program year-round. In Florida, summer walks are unbearable. In Michigan, winter walks require bundling up in coats and boots and dodging ice patches. But in many areas, local malls or community centers offer indoor walking programs that allow people to walk on perfectly level surfaces in comfortable, consistent temperatures, at little or no cost. This makes walking especially easy.

No matter where they live, many people are most comfortable exercising in the privacy of their own homes, using workout videos. Many classic aerobics videos are available. If these seem too strenuous for you, you might try a video that combines walking in place with simple strength training moves designed to give you an all-over workout.

If you like classes, you can find a variety of classes on everything from basic aerobics to water aerobics to spinning in almost every city and town. Whatever your preference, there is a program for you. Don't let the fact that you may live in a place where outdoor activity is not always possible stop you from exercising.

3. Build Your Strength

Aerobic exercises such as walking or biking burn calories, improve cardiovascular function, and keep you upbeat emotionally, but they do not provide much help to fight osteoporosis in the upper body. That requires quick, intense muscle work such as weight lifting, strength training, and sit-ups. The great thing about strength training programs is that they can be done at home with minimal equipment. Many books and videos are available to help you learn how to gain strength. Find one that fits your needs, and keep your bones and muscles strong.

4. **Run or Ride a Bike**

Some people do not enjoy walking. If you know you need exercise, but also know you will not stay enthusiastic about it unless you are moving faster than you can move while walking, I suggest running or biking. A lot of people love biking and it is much easier on the joints than running is. Cities and towns are much better now than they once were about maintaining bike lanes and bike paths. You may find that quite a few errands you now do by car can be accomplished on a bicycle. If you try this, you'll find you can exercise and run many of your errands all at the same time.

5. **Swim**

Some people have physical challenges that make walking or biking difficult or impossible. For these people, and for others, swimming is a great alternative. Many city pools or other facilities offer water aerobics classes or opportunities to swim laps, which is one of the healthiest activities you can do. Swimming takes all the weight off of your body, which means it does not put pressure on your joints. It also works many different muscle groups and provides a gentle cardiovascular workout without joint or bone stress. Indoor pools make swimming a convenient option year-round.

Act on It

Which of the five actions in this key will you take in order to incorporate a consistent exercise program into your life as you move toward greater health? Write them below, commit to them, and start today.

_____

_____

_____

KEY
5

Eat in Balanced Ways

After God created Adam and Eve, He gave them a very simple dining instruction: "You may freely eat of every tree of the garden" (Genesis 2:16). Did He say, "You may freely eat of every Krispy Kreme on the street"? No. Did He say, "You may freely eat of every chip in the bag"? No. He did not tell them to freely eat fast food, frozen pizza, or even low-fat cookies. God told Adam and Eve to eat from the garden. Even though that was centuries ago, long before fast food and microwaves, we would do well to follow His advice.

We have been inundated with an overwhelming amount of bad dietary information from past decades, which has clouded the simple truths of healthy eating: Eat the foods that come from God, as close as possible to the way God made them, and we can't go wrong. We only get in trouble when we corrupt our bodies with foods human beings produce in laboratories and factories. Our bodies were not designed to get nutrition in these forms or from all the added chemicals they include.

Once when I was teaching on the subject of food, I asked the congregation to repeat after me, "I am free to eat!" The looks of fear on people's faces were amazing; they did not really believe the statement I asked them to make. So often people live in bondage to food and food cravings, struggle with weight, and believe for years that they are *not* free to eat! They believe quite the opposite; for them, meals come with rules, regulations, or anxiety. But when too many rules and directives oppress a person's spirit, it longs for freedom. It rebels! This is one reason so many diets fail. They are all about restrictions, and the human spirit is designed for freedom. This is why "I am free to eat!" is such a powerful message and such an unsettling one for some people. They want to believe they are at liberty to eat but have had the opposite message driven into them for too long.

Let me say today: *You are free to eat.* You may not be free to eat everything you want to eat every time you want to eat it, but if you will aim to eat in a healthy, balanced way, you will definitely be free to eat and enjoy!

The Goal: Balance

There's no denying that we love the delicate, creamy tastes of bread, pastries, and other foods made with white flour. And there's no point in even discussing our built-in taste for refined sugar! But these types of foods cause massive insulin responses in our bodies. This is only one reason eating well is so important.

Eating a healthy, balanced diet is not difficult; it is actually easy. It also keeps us obedient to God because the Bible tells us to remain balanced so the devil cannot find an entrance into our lives (1 Peter 5:8). Excess in any area of our lives is the devil's playground, but balance is a spiritually safe and healthy place.

In eating, as in all areas of life, common sense is key. It is not reasonable to think one cookie will bring your health crashing down. Equally unreasonable is the thought that you can eat a full dessert twice every day with no consequences. Moderation is the right path in all things. If you can eat an occasional sweet at a birthday party or a dinner party without overindulging that is a wonderful part of life.

A friend of mine says she absolutely cannot eat even one cookie without eating the whole box, so she knows not to have that first cookie. The Bible says that if your eye offends you, you should pluck it out (Matthew 18:9). What this means is that if one thing in our lives threatens our downfall or causes us major problems, we need to cut it out of our lives. We do not need to go to such extremes most of the time. A little sugar or an occasional pasta will not do irreparable damage to most of us. Most of us are mature enough to mix the occasional indulgence into a general pattern of wholesome, balanced meals.

Look for that balance on your plate. A variety of color is a good sign; it means you are getting a nice mix of vitamins and antioxidants. Allow yourself some carbohydrates for energy—preferably whole-grain ones like brown rice, whole wheat, corn kernels, or beans—but make sure they are balanced by plenty of protein and healthy fat, such as olive oil or avocado. Even if you eat refined carbohydrates, such as sugar or white rice, eating protein and fat at the same time will mix everything in your stomach and delay the rate at which your body absorbs the carbohydrates—resulting in less of a blood-sugar spike. This is why a little ice cream at the end of a meal is a better idea than a donut by itself in the middle of the afternoon.

Due to gluten intolerance some people must stay away from things that contain gluten, but thankfully lots of gluten-free foods are available these days. Learn your own body and make adjustments as needed. Some people cannot eat any sugar due to diabetes or any gluten or any milk products due to allergies. I had a period of about 10 years when I got a headache if I ate beef, so I avoided it. But then my body chemistry changed and now I can eat beef without having a problem. I don't believe that the exact same plan works for everyone. We have to know our bodies and find an eating plan that works for us.

Above all, *don't stress over what you eat.* Realize that healthy eating simply involves rotating a variety of good foods through your week. More than one expert in nutrition has told me that if we eat the same food daily or too frequently we often develop an allergy to it. We need variety and balance. Most foods are good for you! Just don't fall into the American habit of relying too heavily on a few. As long as God's cornucopia crosses your plate each week, and most of it looks more or less like it did when it came from the farm, you will be just fine.

Five Ways to Put Balanced Eating into Practice

1. Make Food Sacred

Learn to do everything you do for God's glory, including eating. Look at your dinner plate and ask if what you are about to eat is mostly what God created for you, basically in its original form. Don't view eating as a secular event that has nothing to do with your spiritual life or your relationship with God. Understand that God is interested in the well-being of your entire body, soul and spirit, and choose to honor Him with what you eat.

I hope you will determine today to make good choices when you eat. Each time you choose good healthy foods, you are choosing life, which is God's gift to you. He wants you to look great and feel great, to be healthy, and to have a good life. You can do these things if you keep in mind that your body is God's temple and that the fuel you put into it determines how well it will operate and for how long.

2. Avoid Refined Carbohydrates

Much of America's soaring rates of obesity and related incidences of heart disease and stroke are caused by the huge amount of refined carbohydrates we eat. They come primarily in the forms of white flour (in bread, crackers, pasta, tortillas, cakes, cookies, donuts, pastries, pretzels), potato (French fries and potato chips), sugar, corn syrup, and other sweeteners. On average, Americans today eat 33 pounds more sugar per year than Americans did about 30 years ago and 64 pounds more grains (mostly white flour) than we did back then. That needs to stop.

How can we make better food choices? Let's make it really simple: Always choose the side salad or the vegetable instead of the fries. Don't eat the rice unless it's brown, and switch to multigrain bread (unless you need gluten-free). None of this is a hardship! Diabetes is a hardship. Having no energy is a hardship. Cancer is a hardship. Good health is easy.

3. Be Fierce About Fruits and Vegetables
Cheap carbohydrates do not provide much nutrition, but they taste good,

so if we do not make an effort to seek out fresh fruits and veggies, our bodies will happily eat themselves sick on fries, bread, and sugar. The best defense is a good offense, and I want you to be *offensive* if that's what it takes to put something decent into your body. For example, base your restaurant choices and dinner menus on vegetables, not meats or breads. I really enjoy restaurants that offer several choices of steamed vegetables. You can also use fruit or raw vegetables to nip hunger in the bud. Gaining weight or becoming unhealthy by eating too many fruits or vegetables is impossible; their water content and fiber prevent that, so eat them aggressively and think of them as armor for your battle against junk food. Here are some more helpful tips.

- Make sure you have at least one fruit or vegetable with *every* meal. Vegetables are even better than fruit because they contain less natural sugar.

- For hors d'oeuvres, serve raw vegetables with a healthy dip.
- Make fruit your snack of choice.
- Don't go more than three hours without eating something. Keeping your blood glucose level stable is wise. Eating often keeps your metabolism working. Be firm about this decision, and if you forget to take healthy snacks with you when you go out, then stop at the grocery store and get some.

4. Replace Saturated Fat and Trans-Fat with Unsaturated Fat

The easiest way to reduce your risk of heart disease is to eat fewer red meats, dairy products, and processed foods made with hydrogenated oils, and to eat more fish, poultry, olive oil, nuts, and avocados. This does not mean you cannot have a steak once in a while, but it does mean you should not eat one daily. Here are several good suggestions.

- Eat fish twice a week for dinner.
- Eat turkey breast or tuna sandwiches instead of roast beef or ham.
- Avoid bacon and sausage. Try turkey sausage as a replacement for pork sausage.
- Use olive oil instead of margarine on bread and instead of mayonnaise in dressings.
- Add nuts and avocados instead of excessive cheese to sandwiches and salads.

5. Balance Your Plate

A typical American dinner plate often includes a huge pile of ribs or fried chicken, a mound of mashed potatoes, a big roll, and a tiny portion of salad or coleslaw trying not to get pushed off the plate. If your goal is to eat a balanced diet, you can still eat all these foods (and whatever else you most enjoy eating); simply change the ratio. That salad or other vegetable (or maybe *two* vegetables) should take up half your plate, while the meat and starch each get a quarter of it. A balanced plate leads to a balanced diet!

Act on It

Which of the five actions in this key will you take so you can choose your foods wisely and eat in a balanced way? Write them below, commit to them, and start today.

_____

_____

_____

KEY
6

Water Your Life

Your body is two-thirds water, just as the earth is two-thirds water and one-third dry land. You and I, and all living creatures, must precisely maintain the water content in our bodies. If it drops below normal, sickness results. Water is so fundamental to our existence that the Bible compares it to the Word of God. We water our bodies with natural water and our souls with the water of God's Word. Ephesians 5:26-27 says, "So that He might sanctify her, having cleansed her by the washing of water with the Word, that He might present the church to Himself in glorious splendor, without spot or wrinkle or any such things."

Just as the water of God's Word cleanses our souls from spiritual filth, so water surrounds and bathes every one of our cells in life-supporting fluid. Water is not only the fluid *around* our cells, it is also the fluid *within* our cells. The water passages of our body transport different nutrients and materials to our cells and remove waste from our cells. They help keep our bodies clean and nourished.

Without water, energy cannot get from our food to our muscles and our brains, waste cannot get cleansed, kidneys cannot function, and the immune system cannot circulate. We cannot cool ourselves either; those little water droplets that get pushed out through the skin as sweat are the body's main system of dumping excess heat.

Everything we do or think depends on the functioning of our cells, and if we want our cells to function at their peak, then providing our bodies with enough water to do its job is essential.

What Happens Without Water?

If a body does not get the water it needs, problems arise. You can go on a hunger strike for a month and suffer no problems worse than a loose wardrobe, but go on a water strike for more than a day and the consequences are severe. Low-level dehydration includes symptoms such as dry, itchy eyes, dry skin that doesn't "snap back" when pulled, constipation, and kidney stones. More serious dehydration begins with nausea, dizziness, and confusion and leads to muscle cramps, kidney failure, and eventually even death.

Even low-grade dehydration has important consequences. When the water level in your body drops, your blood begins to have trouble getting fuel and other nutrients to your cells, so your energy level drops. Your brain cannot run at full power either. You may not even consciously realize you are thirsty, but the evidence is there: fatigue, grumpiness, and poor concentration.

If this sounds like the way you feel every afternoon, then you may not be getting enough water. And if you try to fix your fatigue with coffee or cola, the situation gets worse instead of better: You burn your remaining energy much faster and the coffee leaves you more dehydrated than before because it is a diuretic. The caffeine in coffee and colas is like "low-grade stress in a cup," and offers none of the health benefits of water. If you are prone to afternoon slumps, you would be surprised how quickly you can pull out of them with nothing more than a big glass of water.

Keeping enough water in your body is vital to your health. I encourage you to be proactive about this instead of depending on the feeling of thirst to tell you when you need more water. The sensation of thirst is not always reliable, especially in the elderly. People can get used to feeling all sorts of ways, some of them bad. We can get used to feeling a bit thirsty and dry, but we do not need to let that feeling become familiar and acceptable. I encourage you not to get so used to being thirsty that you do not notice your need for water. Keep your body hydrated all day, every day.

Water and Weight Loss

Believe it or not, drinking water helps tremendously with weight loss, and not being overweight is vital to good health. This is partly because of water's ability to increase metabolism. Drink more water and you will burn a few more calories per hour, regardless of how much you exercise. Water also helps fill your stomach—temporarily. Even though the feeling of fullness will not last, it can make a difference because it slows down your eating and gives your body time to realize it's full before you overeat.

I suspect the reason a lot of people feel the need to snack throughout the day is dehydration rather than low energy. Since mild dehydration registers as fatigue and poor concentration instead of thirst, many people mistake those feelings for hunger. They believe they have "low blood sugar" and need a snack. They end up snacking throughout the day or reaching for the coffeepot again and again, when all they really need is a tall glass of cold water to completely revive them.

But the biggest reason water is a weight loss godsend is that when you drink water, you are not drinking other beverages—sodas, shakes, sweetened iced tea or coffee, energy drinks, juices, and so on. Many of these products are full of sugar, and that certainly won't help the numbers on the scale go down.

I once visited a relative I had not seen in months. She looked great, and I asked if she had lost weight. She had lost 25 pounds. "All I did was start drinking a lot of water," she said. Right there is the simplest diet you will ever see. No changes in meals or exercise at all; simply switch from caloric drinks to water and watch the pounds melt away. If you tend to drink more than a couple of sodas or juices a day, they can easily add up to 20 or 30 pounds a year. You will never find an easier way to improve your health and your waistline than by cutting these unnecessary drinks out of your diet.

How much water do you need? A well-known formula is to take your weight, divide by two, and drink that many ounces of liquid a day. Eight ounces is one cup, so if you weigh 128 pounds, you should be getting eight cups of water a day. If you weigh 160 pounds, you should be getting 10 cups. Not all of this water has to come from actually drinking it. Other liquids count, including the water you get from fruits and vegetables. One of the best things you can do for your body is to make sure it gets the water it needs. I hope you will determine today to stay hydrated to help keep your body working well.

Five Ways to Stay Hydrated

1. Make It Taste Good

Tap water that does not taste good is a serious impediment to drinking eight or more cups of water a day. This task should not be torture for you; it should be pleasant and hassle-free. Do what you have to do to make your water intake something you look forward to; that's the only way you know you will keep doing it. Some ideas:

- Put a filter on your tap.
- Buy bottled water.

- Squeeze a wedge of lemon or lime into every glass.
- Make iced or hot herbal tea.
- There are also many flavored waters available that you can enjoy, but be careful not to get ones with sugar in them.

2. Carry Water Everywhere

You can remind yourself to drink more water, but if it is not handy, you are not likely to do it. Making sure water is always available will go a long way toward establishing the new habit of staying hydrated.

Keep bottles of water in your car, at home, and in your office so you do not even have to think before reaching for them. And when you go to a restaurant and the server pours your glass of water, drink it! Why order another beverage you don't need? In addition, whenever you walk by a water fountain or cooler, take a drink.

3. Have Your Water Call You

If you find it hard to remind yourself to drink a glass of water every hour or two, let technology solve your problem: Set your cell phone to ring every hour as a water reminder! That's one drastic solution to make sure your water is not "out of sight, out of mind." Here are some more:

- Fill a pitcher with ice water in the morning at home or work, wherever you will spend your day, and keep it in front of you as a reminder to drink.
- Keep a water checklist each day. It's easy to lose track!
- Ritualize your water drinking. Tie it to specific times throughout the day as natural reminders. The easiest times are probably mealtimes, but many nutritionists advise against drinking much water during meals because it can dilute your stomach

acid and prevent proper digestion of your food. First thing in the morning is a great time for a glass or two and will help get your metabolism started.

4. Eat Fruit Every Day

Fruit can be 80% water or more, so eating some fruit each day will provide you with the equivalent of an extra glass of water. Some vegetables are also high in water content. You certainly cannot expect to meet your entire fluid requirement through food, but it definitely counts toward that goal.

5. Install Water Coolers

Studies have shown that if people see water coolers, they are more likely to take a drink of water than if they have to get one from the tap. The water cooler functions as a subtle suggestion and people trust they will get good-tasting water from it. If your office does not have a water cooler, suggest installing one. You will help improve the health of the entire office. Coolers work surprisingly well at home too.

Act on It

Which of the five actions in this key will you take so you can stay hydrated and experience the health benefits of water in your life? Write them below, commit to them, and start today.

_____

_____

_____

KEY
7

Be Mindful About Eating

Does any of this sound familiar to you?

- Every time you get a snack out of the refrigerator for your children, you pop a little bit of it in your mouth without even thinking about it—half a piece of cheese, a slice of ham, or a spoonful of peanut butter.
- You have no intention of eating the cake you bake, but you lick clean the batter bowl and the icing knife.
- You get a muffin every day, but throw out half of it "to save calories."
- You don't order dessert because you are on a diet, but you ask your husband for several bites of his.

- You buy miniature candy bars, hide them, and eat just one a day, telling yourself they don't really count because they are so small.

Ring any bells? These are all bad habits I got into in the past through mindlessness. My conscious mind told me that I ate responsibly, and if I looked at my three main meals, I did. But there was a lot of extra eating going on every day that I was not even aware of—finishing off my children's leftovers, sampling food while I cooked, or plundering my husband's desserts.

And those little candy bars! They were so small I figured I could ignore them. Each had only 100 calories, which does not seem like a lot, but I was eating one every single day. Take any unnecessary food you eat every day, divide its calories by 10, and that is how many pounds of difference it can make in a year. Those once-a-day bite-size candy bars were not worth 10 pounds in a year to me, so I stopped eating them.

Also, reading labels on food packaging

has really helped me make better choices. I want to know what I am eating when I eat it!! Sometimes when I see how many calories or how much sugar or sodium is in something I'm about to eat, I decide I don't want it after all.

Think About What You Eat and Drink

We must be mindful about our eating if we are going to take charge of our health. This simply means we think about what we eat and drink, and we make quality decisions about what we put into our bodies. I got rid of my bad food habits by making the commitment that every piece of food I put in my mouth would be a conscious decision.

Never before in human history has so much food been available so cheaply and so often. We stop for gas, and there is food. We go to work, and there is food. There is food in our living rooms, our desk drawers, on airplanes, and in conference rooms.

Part of the problem is that when we see food all around us and see other people eating it, it suddenly seems normal to be munching on something just like everyone else. In addition, the food service industry makes its living off our eating, so they keep suggesting we eat more and more. For example, the employee at the fast-food counter asks us if we would like to try an apple pie with our hamburger (and gets in trouble if he forgets). We are not being rude to refuse something we don't need. We do not need to do anything out of obligation—especially when it comes to eating.

We must keep up our guard against the constant whisper to eat, eat, eat. As I explained in Key 1, few of us can do this by willpower alone, so we need to call on God to help us be mindful at all times. Mindful eating can be as important to good health and a good life as eating the right foods.

What is mindful eating? It's simply being present—really present—whenever we choose to put food or drink in our mouths. It means asking ourselves, "Am I hungry? Do I really want this?" One of the most revealing questions to ask is, "Does this even taste good?"

It can be amazing how often we say "no" to some food we are about to put in our mouths. In fact, the Bible recommends in Romans 13:14 that we make no provision for the flesh and put a stop to thinking about its cravings. Forming the habit of stopping eating the moment you start to feel full is majorly helpful also. You will feel more full in 20 minutes. But if you eat until you feel really full, you will more than likely feel overstuffed by the time all your food gets into your stomach.

Saying "no" to food is something many people have to learn to do because we were taught as children not to waste food. My husband grew up in a family that barely had enough to get by; nobody wasted food. As an adult he felt obligated not only to clean his plate, but to clean our children's plates too. As he got a bit older, he noticed some weight gain and realized he had to stop eating food just because it was there. Instead of eating too much so we do not waste food, we should aim to prepare only what we know we are going to eat. If it is hard for you to leave food on your plate, then use a smaller plate.

Like anything else, mindful eating is a skill that takes practice to perfect. The more you do it, the better you will get, but there will be some bumps along the way. If you keep working at mindful eating, you will get better at it and will find yourself backsliding less and less. But you may still slip now and then, so don't beat yourself up when you do.

Five Ways to Be a Mindful Eater

1. Pay Attention to the Way You Feel After You Eat

I used to think a big plate of pasta was one of my favorite lunches, and I certainly enjoyed it while I was eating it. But about 20 minutes later, an overwhelming sleepiness would come over me. I had no energy for work and felt downright grumpy. When that happened, I did not recover until much later in the afternoon. It took me *years* to connect this with the pasta. Now I know that eating pasta or other starches with little or no protein wrecks me for hours.

How many of your "feeling bad sessions" are connected to bad food you ate earlier that day or the previous evening? Maybe quite a few! Our days are too precious to waste feeling bad, so if you are caught in this trap, please take action. Food is not just about the immediate gratification that comes when some delicious morsel hits your tongue; it's supposed to give you fuel, energy, and a sense of well-being throughout each day. Remember that the good taste on your tongue only lasts a minute or less, and the extra pounds, or lack of energy, can last a long time.

One reason junk food exists is that so many people do not recognize the connection between what they eat and how they feel. Once you become mindful and aware of this, you will be amazed at how you want to change your eating habits. You will actually feel drawn to salads and other healthy foods because you will come to associate them with the good feelings they give you. Even favorites such as chips and cookies may begin to lose some of their appeal and not even taste good anymore as you quickly become aware of your body's negative reaction to them. Our bodies basically crave whatever we give them regularly. You can train your body to like vegetables and not care that much about sugar.

2. Say Grace

Thanking God for the bounty on your table is the best way I know to immediately bring yourself into a healthier relationship with your food. If you have a tendency to overeat, ask God to help you at every single meal to stay in His perfect will. God wants you to enjoy what you eat, and true enjoyment does not mean eating so much that you spend the next few hours feeling sick and guilty.

3. Don't Multitask with Food

When you eat, eat. When you work, work. When you watch TV, don't use that time as a snack break. You will enjoy your life much more if you do one thing at a time and give it your full attention. When something like TV or work distracts you, you get cut off from your natural sensations and are likely to keep stuffing food in your mouth without even knowing it. Many people are so used to having food around that they come to think of it like background noise; it's just there and they eat it without paying much attention to what they are doing. If they are working at their desks without snacking on a bag of jellybeans, something just feels wrong.

Breaking the mindless eating habit is essential. Hundreds or even thousands of calories a day can go into your body and you have little pleasure to show for them. A person can eat four pieces of white bread with butter just because the server set it on the table, not realizing they have eaten 800 to 1,000 calories! Make sure when you are eating that you really are consciously choosing to do so and that you are aware of what you are doing. Most people who eat bread and butter prior to a meal would not even consider or remember it if asked what they ate. They were hungry; the server put it in front of them; and they mindlessly ate it while waiting for the real meal.

4. Slow Down

It takes about 20 minutes for the food you eat to pass through your stomach and reach your small intestine, which detects the food and sends "all full" messages to the brain. But if you are eating quickly, by the time your brain gets those messages from the small intestine, it is too late; a lot more food is already in the pipeline and you are painfully stuffed. Slow down and you give your body more time to fill up. Some tips:

- Chew your food well.
- Swallow one bite before reaching for another.
- Eat several small courses instead of one huge plateful. You will probably feel like you ate more, but in reality you didn't.
- Have relaxed conversation with friends or family while you eat, but never discuss anything intense or upsetting.
- Have your salad first. By the time you get to the calorie-dense main course, you will not be ravenous.
- Don't let yourself get too hungry. When we are really, really hungry, it's hard not to eat too quickly.

5. Turn off the "Bargain" Detector
Americans have become incredibly savvy at getting good deals, whether it's a huge

tub of nuts for five dollars at a bulk dis-
count warehouse or a weekend in Can-
cun for $199. But when we start thinking
like bargain shoppers about our food, we
can get into trouble. All-you-can-eat buf-
fets and salad bars do us no favors. They
plant the notion in our heads that the
more we eat for a low price, the better the
deal. But once we eat beyond what we
need, the only deal we get is a cut rate on
diabetes and cardiovascular disease.

Buying large "family packs" can get
people into trouble too. If you eat a normal portion and freeze the rest of the
package (or have a big family to feed),
great. But if you end up eating more
than you normally would or eating leftovers out of the fridge "before they go
bad," then the good deal is not worth
it. As the old saying goes, "You are what
you eat," and if you don't want "bigger
is better" to apply to your eating habits,
then resist that mentality when you buy
groceries.

Act on It

Which of the five actions in this key will you take so you can practice mindful eating? Write them below, commit to them, and start today.

_____

_____

_____

KEY
8

Curb Your Spiritual Hunger

Wouldn't it be nice if we could control the people and circumstances that are hurtful to us and find a way to avoid pain? Unfortunately, none of us has that kind of control. We do encounter painful situations. We also have to live the lives we have, and through a personal relationship with Jesus Christ we can enjoy our lives, whether all our circumstances suit us or not.

Even though we cannot control the circumstances that affect us, we can control what we put into our bodies. No doubt some of the things we eat, drink, or inhale give us temporary pleasure, comfort, or relief from the emotional pain we feel. Some people put alcohol or drugs into their bodies to try to feel better; others use food for the same purpose.

Most people know about alcohol and drug addictions. But people can just as easily become addicted to food, and food addictions do not carry the same stigma as these other things. Unlike those vices, food has a legitimate—even essential—role in health. Only when it slips into overuse does it become a problem. But getting to that point is really easy.

Food is reliable. Unlike some spouses, friends, or great weather, food is always there. And that's the problem. Anytime we feel emotional pain or spiritual emptiness, whether through sadness, depression, or boredom, we can easily reach for food to numb the pain or fill the void. Before long we mistake our spiritual hunger for physical hunger, and food becomes our immediate solution when we have problems such as not feeling loved, wanted, or confident. The more people try to treat spiritual longings with food or other "feel good" substances, the greater their souls' cry for spiritual nourishment will be and the greater their discomfort or *dis-ease* will be.

Thankfully, we have another source of comfort that is always there when we need it. Unlike junk food or drugs, it does not leave people overweight, sick, or lethargic. It doesn't even cost anything. That something is God. He is called the "Father of sympathy (pity and mercy) and the God [Who is the Source] of every comfort (consolation and encouragement), who comforts (consoles and encourages) us in every trouble" (2 Corinthians 1:3-4).

When I hurt, I have learned to run to God first instead of to another person or to a substance. It took me years to learn to do this, and I still sometimes have to remind myself under certain circumstances that what I really need is spiritual nourishment. Developing this habit has been very good for me and it will be for you too. It will do more to keep your mind and body sound and your life on an even keel than anything I know. Your spirit needs nourishment just as your body does. I encourage you not to wait until you have a crisis in your life to start feeding your spirit and to make a decision today to grow in your spiritual health and strength, just as you are improving your physical well-being.

Today's Spiritual Famine

Today more people than ever before are spiritually malnourished. Too many things in our society distract people from the things of God and encourage them to concentrate on material life instead. People get caught up in making money to buy bigger homes and spiffier cars or to keep up with the latest trends. Families are less likely to live close together, which removes another important spiritual support structure. Time for church and religious matters, even spending peaceful time in nature, gets pushed aside by busy schedules and entertainment. The quiet voice of God gets drowned out by the constant drone of the television set or by excessively trying to keep up with Facebook friends.

I am certainly not immune to the temptations I have mentioned. I live my daily life in the spiritual realm, but I have a job running an international ministry and that can leave me just as exhausted as other people's jobs can leave them. Those of us in the ministry have committed to lay our lives down to serve others, and we gladly do so, but that does not mean it is easy or exciting every single day. I have to stick really close to God to keep my spirit nourished and to draw my enthusiasm from Him.

No matter what people do for a living or what they feel their calling is in life, *everyone* needs to stick close to God. He is the only one who can give us the comfort, relief, and strength we need. If we try to fill our need for God with anything else, including food, we will continue to feel empty and dry. Many addictions come from being spiritually hungry. Even food addictions may actually be rooted in spiritual issues, not in any sort of physical hunger. Some of the classic signs of food addiction are the following:

- Binging or binging and purging.
- Making deals with yourself about an addiction. For example, "If I can just eat these cookies today, I will run three miles tomorrow."

- Lying to yourself or others about how much you have eaten or about your eating habits.
- Eating as an immediate reaction to stress.
- Unhealthy eating that starts after the death of a loved one, the loss of a job, the end of a relationship, or some other traumatic event.
- Eating when you do not have anything else to do.
- Feeling that no activity is complete unless accompanied by food.
- Feeling worse instead of better after eating.

Why Bother?

If you have identified a lack of spiritual nourishment in your life, why would you want to fix it? What good would it do to get the spiritual food you need? How could growing spiritually help you kick an addiction? Let me explain.

If you have a rich spiritual life, you will be satisfied with the moments and experiences of your life and will not need to supplement those moments with any kind of food. Think about it. When you walk through a field on a summer night and see the fireflies, isn't that a fulfilling moment? When you hold your new baby or grandbaby for the first time, that is a rich, fulfilling moment. You do not even think, *It's nice to hold this baby, but I would feel better if I had a donut.* No, you are in awe and you are completely satisfied, maybe even overwhelmed with joy. That moment is complete in itself; you need nothing else.

When you receive the spiritual nourishment you need, you will be thoroughly and deeply satisfied. All your moments will be complete and you will not need to supplement them. You will not feel that you lack or crave anything, and you will have no problem eating and drinking only what your body really needs.

Five Ways to Nourish Your Spirit

1. Be Honest

The first step to receiving God's love and true fulfillment is to stop denying to yourself (or others) that your problem is a spiritual one. You cannot lie to God anyway, so why bother trying to deceive yourself? For years I was addicted to cigarettes, but I told myself I kept smoking to stay thin; I did not admit to myself that I was addicted to nicotine. Truth is the way to spiritual fulfillment and freedom, and now is the time to start. If you need to, admit to yourself that your spirit is not getting what it needs from life. Once you do, God will show you how to change that.

Some questions that will help you be honest with yourself: Who are you? Do you love and accept yourself? What are your core values? Do the things in your life—the people, your job, and so on—support those values, or do they keep you separated from your true self? Try to identify the sources of the emptiness that drives you to eat, smoke, drink alcohol excessively, or overwork. What imbalances are these things creating in your life? What can you do to start filling those empty areas with activities or people that will help feed your spirit and connect you with God?

Doing things you know are wrong is a big source of depression and discontentment. Ask God to help you be honest with yourself and with Him as you begin breaking the power of addictions in your life and finding your fulfillment and joy in Him instead of in other things.

2. Ask

God loves you very much and wants to help you, but He also wants you to ask for His help. A man once told me that when he feels overwhelmed, he lifts one hand toward Heaven and says, "Come help me, Jesus." That really helps him. We all need to realize God hears the faintest cry of our hearts. We can stop trying so hard to do everything on our own and ask Him for help.

The next time you are tempted to eat because you are upset or sad, say "no" out loud. Then go sit quietly for a moment and ask God to help you in your situation. You will be amazed at how much difference asking makes.

God's grace is always available to partner with our choice, and He responds to our sincere requests for His help. As we choose to do what is right and lean on Him to give us strength, His power enables us to follow through and experience victory.

3. Crowd Out Bad Habits

Bad habits need room to operate. Not much—they're pretty clever—but we can learn to give them no place to take up residence in our lives. One good strategy for keeping bad habits at bay is to recognize what your temptations are and then set up your life in such a way that they have no room to operate. Fill your life with so many positive, spiritually reaffirming things that there is no room for anything else. Praying regularly about temptations and not waiting until you're tempted is wise, and an aggressive battle plan. Jesus said we should pray that we "come not into temptation." He didn't say to pray that we would never be tempted. Temptation is part of life, but aggressive praying can keep it from overwhelming us.

4. Support Programs

Breaking the habit of anesthetizing your spiritual hunger with food or other substances can be really tough. Many people find the road easier if they have the support of a group of people who have been there, can identify with how hard it is, and are trying to walk the same path. Several good programs are available throughout the country to help people break their addictions. They teach people to admit that without God

they are powerless over the addiction, to
believe that only God can restore them
to health, and to make the decision to
turn their will and life over to His care.
Not everyone is comfortable finding
spiritual nourishment through groups,
but many who were skeptical at first
have found success this way. If you find
yourself struggling alone for a break-
through, give a group a try.

5. Give It Some Time

Instant success rarely happens, so don't
plan on it. When you first separate from
a destructive behavior, you will feel there
is a void in your life. You have become so
used to wrong behavior as a part of your
daily existence that you do not quite feel
like yourself once it's gone, even if you
know you are better off.

Don't worry. Change is always rough
at first. As you may have heard, breaking a bad habit takes about 30 days.
Focus on the good habit you are forming instead of the bad one you are

breaking. Commit fiercely to success, but love yourself no matter what happens. You will have some slips, but you will have more successes. If you maintain faith in God and believe that you can do it, suddenly a day will come, perhaps weeks later, when you realize that things are much easier for you. You no longer consciously have to try so hard. You have curbed your spiritual hunger at last and broken the addictive cycle in your life.

Act on It

Which of the five actions in this key will you take to curb your spiritual hunger and get your spiritual needs met? Write them below, commit to them, and start today.

_____

_____

_____

KEY
9

De-Stress

There's a dangerous drug in our society. Here's what just a little bit of it will do to you: It sends your heart into overdrive, pounding at four times its natural rate. It does the same to your lungs. It constricts your blood vessels and raises your blood pressure to dangerous levels. It dries your mouth and shuts down your stomach and intestines. It drains the blood from your face and skin. It scrambles your immune system. It wrecks your sleep, turns off sexual interest and reproductive capability, slows healing, and increases your risk of periodontal disease, skin disease, and autoimmune diseases. It shuts down short-term memory and rational thought. It actually shrinks part of your brain. And it even makes you overeat.

Sounds like bad news, doesn't it? I bet you would go out of your way to steer clear of this drug. Yet you give yourself doses of it every day. I was addicted to it for years. The drug is cortisol, the most famous of the glucocorticoids—the stress drugs. And your body makes them daily.

Stressed Out

When we say "I've had a stressful day" or "I'm stressed out," we mean we cannot relax. Things come up during the day, or carry over from previous days, that we must deal with. If enough of those things happen or go unresolved, then we have no escape, no place to relax, and we are "stressed out."

Stress is the opposite of relaxation. Physically, stress is the body's gearing up to tackle whatever situation arises. It does this by sending stress hormones in all directions. When a stressful situation happens, out of your adrenal glands come cortisol and the other glucocorticoids. Out of your brain comes adrenaline (which scientists call *epinephrine*) and related hormones, which are messengers that rush through the body telling all your systems— your heart, muscles, skin, and others—what to do. In the case of stress, the message is "Get ready for action," also known as the "fight or flight" response.

In itself, fight or flight is not a bad thing. It is a great system if you have to save a child from a burning building or run from a hungry bear. You get hyper-alert, super-quick, and you rescue the child or leave the bear far behind. After a few minutes, your heartbeat comes down and life goes on.

You will be glad you have this system the next time you face an emergency, but the human body was never designed for twenty-first-century living, when mentally stressful moments are the norm, not the exception. All the changes that cortisol and the other stress hormones cause in our bodies help a lot in the short term, but can make us very, very sick—even kill us—if they happen every day. And in a typical modern life, they often happen not just every day but every hour.

A Guide to Stress-Related Disease

Occasional stress is healthy, even stimulating. However, chronic stress does not ever allow the body to recover and slowly kills it because it increases the possibility of sickness or other poor health conditions. Let's take a look at the different diseases stress causes or aggravates.

Cardiovascular Disease

Perhaps the most important way stress affects your body is to increase the rate at which blood pumps through it. That's the only way to get fuel—glucose and oxygen—to your muscles where it's needed (or where your body assumes it's needed). To do this, your heart beats more rapidly and your blood vessels constrict to force blood through them faster. This means your blood pressure gets very high during stress. That is fine if it happens only occasionally, like during exercise. But if you are stressed all the time, then that elevated blood pressure stays too high for too long. Not good.

High blood pressure increases the pounding on the walls of your blood vessels (especially at the Y's where a blood vessel branches into two). As soon as the cells that make up those walls become loose, material in your blood can get under them and stick to the wall, forming a blockage. Such blockages cause heart attacks and strokes. No surprise, then, that people with heart disease are *four times* as likely to have heart attacks if they also suffer from high stress.

Diabetes

When your body senses the alarm from your stress hormones, it wants to send as much fuel as possible to your muscles. Where does the fuel come from? From your fat reserves. Adrenaline signals your fat cells to send their fat into your bloodstream, where it can be converted into glucose for your muscles to use as needed. During stressful times, your body tries to keep as much fat and glucose in your blood as possible. To do this, it overrides your insulin, which is trying to force the fat and glucose into storage or muscle tissue. (The only places it does not override the insulin are in muscles being used right then, which need all the glucose they can get.) Since insulin resistance is a diabetic's main problem, you can see why stress makes it much worse.

Compounding the problem, your blood gets thicker during stress. Extra platelets get added to your blood, and platelets are responsible for making blood clot. Blood that clots easily is what you want if your stomach is about to get sliced open by a surgeon's knife or a bear claw, but not if you have diabetes or heart disease, because it is more likely to create blockages.

Weight Gain

During the first few minutes of a stressful situation, the adrenaline from your brain suppresses hunger. But the cortisol from your adrenal glands actually stimulates appetite, and cortisol takes longer than adrenaline to circulate through your body and get removed, so you end up hungry.

Cortisol's job is to take over after you have dealt with an immediate threat. It keeps your muscles and senses on high alert for a while because the threat might still be around, and it tells you to *eat*. Since you probably expended a lot of energy in fight or flight mode, you now need to fuel up to be ready for the next emergency. Cortisol makes you ravenous and makes fat storage extra easy—especially around the abdomen.

You probably know the scenario. You have a high-stress job, and for nine or more hours a day you run around at an extremely fast, focused pace, hardly thinking about food. You may even skip lunch. No time! Then, finally, you trudge home at 8:00 p.m. with Chinese takeout and practically inhale it. The stress is gone (temporarily), you're unwinding, your cortisol is still going strong, and now it tells you to eat the whole chicken chow mein, plus dessert, and store those calories fast. This is why chronic stress is one of the main culprits of weight gain.

Ulcers and Digestive Disorders

The slow process of converting food in your stomach to energy does not fall under the "emergency" category, so when faced with stress, your body shuts down digestion. When stress comes into your life, blood gets diverted from the stomach and small intestine to the heart and other muscles. Then, once the stress disappears, cortisol cranks up digestion again.

Normally, your stomach wall is lined with a thick layer of mucus to protect it from the hydrochloric acid that breaks down food in the stomach. But when stress frequently shuts down your digestion, your body can get out of sync as it makes mucus to coat the stomach. Then the acid burns a hole in an unprotected spot on the stomach wall, and you have a painful ulcer.

Your intestines also suffer when you are under stress. While stress shuts down the stomach and small intestine, it actually speeds up the movement of the large intestine to unload excess baggage in preparation for any "flight" that may be necessary. When the stress goes away, this process is reversed. But just like throwing your car back and forth between "drive" and "reverse" can mess up your transmission, regular on-and-off stress throws your intestines out of whack. They can spasm, causing or aggravating such conditions as colitis and irritable bowel syndrome (IBS).

Immunity

When stress hits, your body makes extra white blood cells to fight infection. And cortisol pulls your existing white blood cells from their everyday tasks, such as looking for cancer cells, and sends them to the front lines to protect against infection from any puncture wounds you might suffer during the stress. This is kind of like your body's version of mobilizing the National Guard. After about a half-hour of stress, cortisol starts reducing the number of white blood cells you have in circulation. Why? If you keep those National Guard white blood cells on alert, racing around the body looking for enemies and there aren't any enemies, eventually they start mistaking your *own cells* for enemies and attacking them. This results in autoimmune disease—your own immune system attacking you.

Cortisol simply tries to do its job by reducing the number of white blood cells when you are under stress. But there's a problem. If the stress goes on for a while, cortisol keeps reducing your white blood cells until your immune system is depleted. With such low immunity, you are suddenly more likely to catch colds and other diseases.

As with so many other systems in your body, a bit of stress is not bad for your immune system. During the first few minutes of a stressful situation, you feel a quick burst of energy and are less likely to get infections or colds. But soon, your white blood cell count starts to fall and it keeps on falling the longer the stress goes on, resulting in a severely compromised immune system.

General Aging

We have all seen what happens to people who suffer through years of stress. Their hair turns gray. Their skin becomes sallow and wrinkly. Everything from their eyes to their muscle tone just looks "not quite right." By now, you should understand why. Cortisol tells the body to drop all long-term projects and put its resources into short-term survival.

One of the longest-term projects in the body is the general cell repair that goes on all the time and helps keep people looking and feeling young. Your body uses the protein in your diet to repair these cells and the DNA in the cells. Under chronic stress, your body stops repairing its cells and instead uses the protein as an extra source of fuel for "fight or flight." All maintenance projects cease. This explains why people undergoing long-term stress look run down. They are breaking down on a cellular level. Lowering stress, regular exercise, and healthy eating will slow down the aging cycle and you can look younger than you actually are instead of older than you are.

Other Conditions

Think of anything bad that can happen to the body and stress will intensify it. Stress causes depression by throwing off your serotonin levels. It makes your muscles tense (which is useful if you are preparing for fight or flight), which leads to everything from back pain to migraines (caused by tense head muscles). As I mentioned earlier, it turns off higher brain functions and memory to let you concentrate on quick, instinctive reactions to stress; furthermore, chronic stress actually *shrinks* the part of the brain that houses memory. It increases periodontal disease because your immune system does not fight as well against the germs that cause the disease; it slows growth in children; it inhibits reproduction in both women and men.

One obvious consequence of stress is that it makes sleep very difficult. Sleep is pretty much the opposite of stress. To sleep, you must relax, and relaxation is almost impossible with all that cortisol racing through your blood, accelerating your heart rate and lungs.

But lack of sleep in itself causes many of the same conditions stress does. So the result is a vicious circle of stress causing poor sleep, and poor sleep causing more stress.

It's time to get yourself out of that vicious circle! Today, if you want to live without dangerous stress loads, you must make a choice to do so. You will need to know what to do and how to do it. Here are some ideas to get you started.

Five Ways to De-Stress Yourself

I find that many people nod their heads and give lip service to the idea that stress is bad and should be reduced in their lives, but they do not do much about it. I hope my explanations in this chapter make very clear to you that stress is not an inconvenience; stress is deadly. You *cannot* lead a full and righteous life if stress is breaking your emotions and your spirit.

I know what I am talking about. For years, I was ruined by stress. I was sick and extremely tired all the time. My schedule was

insane and my mind never stopped churning.
I did so much every day and worked so late
every night that I could not get my system
to calm down enough to sleep properly. I got
emotionally upset on a regular basis. Most of
the time I was stressed about my schedule,
yet I was the one making that schedule, so
I had no one to blame but myself. I was the
only one who could change my schedule, but
it took years of misery to get me to the point
of being willing to do so.

When I finish ministering at a conference,
I'm tired physically, mentally, and emotionally.
For years, I came away from meetings where
the Spirit of God moved in great power, and I
went home and had a bad attitude. I felt sorry
for myself, got angry, and took it out on the
people around me, all of which is ungodly
behavior.

Now, after a conference, I take some time
to eliminate stress. I always rest, but I might
also do it by treating myself to something I
really enjoy. I get a good healthy, hot meal.
I might purchase something pretty or watch
a good clean movie, while holding my dog

and petting her. Sometimes I'll get a massage because it is a great stress reliever. Whatever it is, I know I will not go back to work until I have eliminated the stress of my responsibilities at the conference. I want to teach God's Word for the rest of my life, which I pray will be long. In order to do that I know I need to have regular de-stress periods in my life. It has become a necessity for me instead of an option. I actually feel that I am sinning if I don't rest regularly because I know what it does to my body and overall health and I believe I should glorify God with my whole being!

That's just one example from my life. I can think of many others, and I am sure you already know of ways that work for you—though whether you actually do them is another matter. Now that you know how sick stress can make you, the next time you feel your body start to work itself into a frenzy, I hope you will try something that will relieve it. Here are some classic, tried-and-true methods.

1. Social Support

Studies show that social isolation leads to elevated cortisol levels. We are social beings, and spending time around other people that we enjoy is one of the best ways to make us feel good and relaxed. Various social outlets are right for different people; just make sure that you have *some*. My suggestions:

- Family and friends
- Church
- Groups and clubs

2. Shrug Therapy

There are some things you can control in life—your choice of job, your friends, your coffee intake, and the amount of sleep you get. There are others you can't control—what people say and do, the fluctuations of the stock market, or the flat tire you got this morning. How you react to things you cannot control helps determine your stress level and quality of health. People who regularly get upset over minor things suffer in many ways. People who shrug them off do a lot better. The Bible calls this "casting your care," which simply means letting God handle your problems instead of wrestling with them by yourself (1 Peter 5:7).

Shrugging something off does not mean you are ignoring it or being indifferent to it; it just means acknowledging there is nothing you can do to change the situation at that particular moment. The flat tire has already happened. Dealing with it by calling AAA makes sense; throwing a tantrum and kicking the tire does not.

The low-stress approach to life is to shrug things off. Life happens. God works in mysterious ways. If you trust Him to work things out, you will navigate the dips of life with barely a blip in your cortisol level, and that will keep you healthy and at peace.

3. Find Your Element—and Stay There

My husband once did one of the wisest things I have ever seen. Before he and I entered full-time ministry, he worked as an engineer. One time, he was offered a promotion that included a pay raise and a lot of prestige. But he turned it down.

Dave explained that he had watched the other men in that position. They had to travel extensively and were constantly saddled with unreasonable deadlines that put them under tremendous stress. "That's not the way I want to live," Dave said.

Instead, Dave chose a position that allowed him to stick to his core values— commitment to family and comfort with self—rather than chasing corporate power so others would look up to him.

Why would anyone choose a higher paycheck just to spend it on doctor bills to relieve job-related, stress-induced illnesses? Job stress causes as much illness in this country as overeating and lack of exercise. Like those things, it kills.

We all want more money, and then we get it and find it does not change the basic dynamics of our lives much. Maybe we drive fancier cars or eat in better restaurants, but we are still the same basic people and our happiness level does not really increase. The most important foundations of long-term happiness are being in right relation-ship with God, good health, a loving home life, work that is satisfying and not overly stressful, and enough money to not have to worry about finances. Everything else is gravy. Money is an important consideration and can make some things in life easier, but I would advise people not to take any job purely for the money if it will make them stressed or less happy on a daily basis.

You may be in a position that does not make you happy and you need to make a change. You may be proud of your position, but if it steals your health, consider getting out as fast as you can. If your superiors constantly disrespect or dishonor you, either work it out with them or think about finding employment elsewhere. Whatever is causing you high stress, do your best to eliminate it so you can avoid the negative effects stress will have on your health and on your life.

I believe there could be much more happiness and less stress in the world if people would take time to figure out their natural elements and stay there. Your element is waiting for you somewhere; if you are not in it, go find it. Jesus came so that we may "have life, and have it to the full" (John 10:10, NIV). Do whatever you need to do to make sure you fully enjoy the life He has provided for you.

4. Nutrition, Supplements, and Diet

What you physically put into your body has a huge impact on your stress level. The most obvious example is caffeine. A cup of coffee is a cup of stress—it speeds your breathing and heart rate, tenses your muscles, hones your senses, and so on. Nothing else has the immediate and obvious effect on stress that caffeine does, but other aspects of nutrition can be very important in regulating your stress. A cup of coffee, or perhaps two a day, is not bad in itself, but you need to eat properly and do other things to enhance your health. I can remember when I drank seven or eight cups of coffee each day and smoked a pack and a half of cigarettes. I went most of the day without eating and then ate a big meal at night. I was always on some kind of crash diet. At that time in my life, although I was a Christian, I was spiritually deficient and I lived by emotions. No wonder I felt bad a lot. When I went to the doctor hoping for a pill that would make me feel better, he always told me my problem was too much stress. This diagnosis always made me angry because I didn't want to admit that I was not doing a good job of managing my life.

One of the first things I did to help myself was start taking nutritional supplements and vitamins. I also studied stress, nutrition, food, rest, and other aspects of managing my health. I learned that a high-protein diet avoids the mood-thumping effect of surging and crashing blood sugar brought on by a high-carb diet. Nutritional supplements and vitamins are also important. By revving up your metabolism, stress causes you to burn through certain vitamins at a furious pace, particularly vitamin C and the B vitamins. If you are under heavy stress, make sure you get extra doses of these in your food or through supplements. You may need to experiment to find the right nutritional supplements for yourself. Varying opinions exist about the safety and effectiveness of many over-the-counter herbs and supplements. While they have been safe for me, you should consult your physician before trying them, and make sure if you do take them that they contain high-quality, good ingredients.

5. Relaxation Techniques

Relaxation is not selfish. It is not slacking off. It is a way of recharging your batteries—physically, emotionally, and spiritually—so you can resume your responsibilities at full-strength tomorrow. You will accomplish more during your days, live longer and healthier, and enjoy life more if you take time to treat yourself right. There are many ways to do this. Here are some favorites:

- **Play.** Adults need to play just as much as children do, and for the same reasons. Play is a terrific way to relax; you get the fun of creativity and challenge without the pressure, because there are no "repercussions" based on your performance. Choose a play activity that is flat-out fun for you and that is a total distraction and escape from the rest of your life.

- **Laugh.** "A cheerful heart is good medicine," says the Bible, "but a crushed spirit dries up the bones" (Proverbs 17:22, NIV). Laughing good-naturedly at yourself and at life's ups and downs is a great stress-reduction practice. Make your next book or video one that makes you laugh out loud; life can't be drama all the time.
- **Exercise.** I have already discussed exercise in depth, so I won't say much here. Just know that it is probably the single best way to burn off stress.
- **Sleep.** In the beginning of the world, God divided the light from the darkness and made day and night. This is because there is a time to work and a time to sleep. We are meant to stop each day and take some time to rest and recharge. Do not try to steal from this time—embrace it. Your body will actually tell you what it needs if you listen to it. My body certainly tells me when it is

tired. For years I ignored it. I pushed
and pushed and pushed until finally
my body said, "I am tired of being
pushed beyond reasonable limits. I
am not going to cooperate anymore."
And it broke down. Now when my
body lets me know it needs to rest,
I rest. If it is sleepy, I take a nap.
Sometimes 10 minutes is enough to
refresh me. Getting proper sleep and
rest will do wonders to reduce the
stress in your life.

- **Prayer.** Prayer is simply talking to
God. Some people find time with
God in the morning or evening to be
the best method for nurturing calm
and focus, but you can try it in mini-
bursts too. Any time things start to
feel overwhelming at work (or anywhere else, for that matter), stop
and ask God to refresh you. Take a
few deep breaths and let your mind
calm down. Be deliberate about this
because it will do a lot to relieve your
stress and restore your peace. Talk to

God all throughout the day about everything. He is interested in every aspect of your life and all that concerns you.

- **Massage.** Nothing makes me feel better than a massage. And feeling good is health in itself! Massage not only relieves and tones sore muscles, but also lowers blood pressure and heart rate, releases endorphins in the brain, pushes toxins out of muscles, promotes blood flow, and increases relaxation.

- **Other ideas.** Unwind with music, take a warm bath by candlelight, or walk through a forest in autumn. You know what relaxation feels like, and you know when it's happening to you. Different people relax in different ways. Dave relaxes by playing golf and my son enjoys snowboarding, but neither of those would help me relax at all. Discover what relaxes you and make relaxing on purpose part of your daily life. Above all, monitor your emotional state. Your emotions are valid, and if they feel out-of-whack, they need some TLC from you.

Act on It

Which one of the five actions in this key will you take so you can reduce the stress in your life? Write them below, commit to them, and start today.

_____

_____

_____

KEY
10

Live with the Right Vision

To get anywhere, you have to know where you are going. You may not know the exact route to take, but you at least have a goal in mind. If you are driving from St. Louis to New Orleans, you have a goal and lots of ways to achieve it, from GPS systems to reading maps to stopping and asking directions. On the other hand, if you simply get in your car in St. Louis and drive with no idea where you are going, you will likely end up getting lost and perhaps far away from your desired destination.

Before any of us can achieve victory in any area of our lives, we have to transition from "wishing" to taking action. In your effort to enjoy the good and healthy life you deserve, you'll need to have a vision of your goal. To develop that vision, you can start by asking yourself questions such as these: "What will my life be like when I am eating well, and I feel fit, comfortable, and happy?" "What will I look like?" And, "What kinds of activities will fill my days?" Only when you have a vision of the new you can you start making the necessary plans to achieve it. Ask yourself if your current actions will help you reach your desired destination, and be honest in your evaluation.

God wants you to start progressing toward your goals, but before you can do that you must get a clear image of the good future He has in store for you and of the goals that will help you get there. If you focus on your past disappointments and let them influence you in negative ways, you will have a very hard time escaping them. I want to encourage you to talk about your future, not your past. Talk about the new you that you are becoming.

Every successful person starts by envisioning his or her success. We all need a dream to reach for. If you can develop the right vision for your life, you can achieve it. Now that you have learned in this book the tools you need to become a success inside and out, to look like one and feel like one and to have good health and a good life, it's time to develop the vision you need for your life and determine where you are headed from this moment on. Here are five ideas to help you.

Five Ways to Develop Right Vision

1. Think (and Speak) Your Reality into Existence

"Manifesting your reality" sounds like something from a contemporary self-help course, but the concept actually comes straight from the Bible, in Proverbs 23:7: "As he thinks in his heart, so is he." I like to say it this way: "Where the mind goes, the man follows." Positive thoughts are precursors to a positive life.

What you think is up to you. You can choose your own thoughts and should do so carefully because they have creative power. Thoughts become words and actions. If we do not reject bad thoughts, we will ultimately turn those thoughts into bad words and actions that are not pleasing to God. The same principle applies to good thoughts. If we embrace them, they will lead to positive words and actions.

We have more to do with the way our lives turn out than we like to admit. Learning how to think right is mandatory for good health. Thoughts affect emotions, and thoughts and emotions both affect the body. When we begin to think and speak in healthy, right ways, we help ourselves move toward the vision God has given us for our lives.

I encourage you to make a decision right now to have a healthy mind that thinks right thoughts. Renewing your mind will take some time and effort. You will have to learn new, positive ways to think, but those new ways will be the keys to a great future. One of the best ways I know to think right thoughts is to read and meditate on God's Word. If you allow His Word to shape your thoughts, it will also shape your life.

Another excellent practice is to create a vision of the ideal you. Carry this vision around in your head and assume the role of the ideal you as though you were acting in a play. Say and do the things the "ideal you" would do, instead of what the "now you" does. Soon you will become this ideal person and will not be acting anymore. If you have never been a disciplined person but you would like to be, then stop saying, "I'm just not disciplined," and begin saying, "I am a disciplined person." Where your physical well-being is concerned, say, "I look great, I feel great, and I eat right. I love to exercise and I have an abundance of energy."

Start by doing a word sketch. Describe your ideal self's activities, physical appearance, values, and so on. Make it concrete, so it feels as real as possible. Writing down your goals helps bring them into the real world and make them solid. Keep your vision and a list of your goals handy so you can consult it periodically to see how you are doing.

Your list of goals can serve as stepping-stones on your way to becoming your ideal self. Set goals that focus on healthy living and on your well-being. For example, "I will lose 20 pounds" is not a healthy goal because it puts the emphasis on the scale instead of your lifestyle. "I will control my portions and get daily exercise" is a great goal, and losing five pounds this month as a result is a fine short-term goal. Make sure your goals are part of a healthy vision and you will be well on your way to a healthy life.

2. Manage Your Feelings

We all have emotions and must learn to manage them. Emotions can be positive or negative. They can make us feel wonderful or awful. They can make us excited and enthusiastic or sad and depressed. They are a central part of being human, and that is fine. Unfortunately, most people live according to how they feel. And that is not fine, because feelings are not wisdom.

God has given us wisdom, and we should walk in that, not in our emotions. Wisdom includes common sense; it involves making choices now, based on the knowledge we currently have, that we will be satisfied with later. Wisdom includes discernment, prudence, discretion, and many other great qualities.

The healthier we are, the more we can walk in wisdom because the more stable our emotions will be. Healthy people can handle disappointment easier than those who are unhealthy. They can remain stable through the storms of life. But when people's bodies are already drained, their emotions cave in at the first sign that anything is going wrong. When I was eating poorly, not sleeping, and living under constant stress, I was dominated by my emotions. I have learned firsthand that when emotions have been under a lot of strain, they need time to heal just as a broken bone or other injury would.

It seems to me sometimes that many people in the world are angry and many more are sad. Things are pretty bad when people have to go to classes for "road rage." I have come to believe part of this emotional epidemic may be dietary. Most people simply do not realize that their emotional well-being is connected to what they eat. Thank God we no longer have to be like "most people." Through proper education and a desire for a lifetime of health, we can be released from bondage into healthy, happy, peaceful lives.

To manage our emotions and our lives, we need to call on Heaven's wisdom; but to have the clarity of mind to receive Heaven's wisdom, it helps to have a healthy body based on good nutrition.

3. Assume the Best

We can quickly ruin a day with wrong thinking. Friendships are destroyed because of wrong thinking. Business deals go wrong. Marriages fail. It's so easy to concentrate on everything that is wrong instead of what is right about a person or a situation. When we do that, we soon find ourselves wanting to get away from those people or circumstances when what we really need is to escape our own negative minds.

We need to replace suspicion and fear with trust. Trust breeds more trust. Trusting others, and especially trusting God, helps keep us healthy in every aspect of our being. When we trust, we are relaxed and at rest.

This is good old common sense. Consider the following example. You are walking down an unfamiliar street and an angry man comes out of his house with a pit bull growling on a leash and mutters, "What are you doing in my yard?" You think, *Who is this angry person?* and you act angry and suspicious right back, telling him to mind his own business. His unfriendliness boomerangs back to him and probably makes him even less friendly. Your behaving the same way he did does not help anyone. On the other hand, if you can somehow look beyond his suspicions (maybe he was recently robbed or has encountered a great tragedy in his life) and act friendly and relaxed toward him, more often than not he will relax too, and you will have a pleasant interaction that improves his day and yours.

4. Get the Little Things Right

Have you ever gone out to breakfast with someone whose meal cost eight dollars and watched him torture himself over the tip? He has two one-dollar bills in change, but he thinks leaving just a dollar would be chintzy. Yet does he leave two dollars? No. He decides that would be too much. Instead, he wastes 10 minutes of his life getting change for that second dollar so he can leave $1.50 tip and save 50 cents, rather than leave an "exceptionally generous" tip of two dollars.

What would happen if he left the full two dollars? He would free up some valuable time—time undoubtedly worth more than 50 cents. And he would make the server's day. Not that the actual 50 cents means much to the server either, but the message that goes along with that 50 cents means the world! It says thanks, and it communicates that the waitperson's work has value. Maybe this message gets lost— the wait staff may just sweep up the tip without counting it—but the generous person will always be blessed. He will know instinctively that he has done the better thing. What an opportunity! We can increase the happiness of others and ourselves for mere pocket change!

This is just one tiny example of the many ways little things have surprisingly powerful repercussions. Small things set the tone for our days. Going the extra mile for people—whether with a slightly larger tip, an unexpected compliment or gift, or even holding a door open—costs us very little and gets us a lot.

There are many other ways to get the little things right. Do all the small things that a person of sincerity, faith, self-respect, and excellence would do. Do the thing that Jesus would do!

5. Be a Part of Something Bigger Than Yourself

You will have much more success in all your endeavors if you make them about something other than *you*. Nothing can make your vision more "right" than knowing you are living for God's glory and in the power of His Spirit. Whether it is working with those less fortunate than you, helping children become strong and happy adults, or spreading the Good News far and wide, nothing is more fulfilling or makes doing the right thing easier than knowing that you are part of the grandest vision of all.

Act on It

Which of the five actions in this key will you take so you can develop the right vision and goals for your life? Write them below, commit to them, and start today.

_____

_____

_____

KEY
11

Make It Easy

Congratulations! You have made it through the most challenging parts of the book, and you are still going. You now have the tools and tips you need to create a good life with good health, inside and out. If you are a person of passion, like I am, you are probably chomping at the bit to launch into your new lifestyle, to embrace all of it as fast as possible. If that is the case, then my purpose in writing this book has been fulfilled.

But let me be the first to say, "*Whoa!*" Go slowly. If you put down this book, pull on your sneakers, and try to start walking five miles a day while making a free-range chicken stir-fry for dinner, guzzling eight glasses of water, and reading five chapters of the Bible each day you will probably be overwhelmed.

Most human beings want everything fast, but God is not in a hurry. He is in this with you for the long haul. He will deliver you from all your bondages little by little (Deuteronomy 7:22). It takes a long time to get our lives into a mess, and it will take some time to see things turn around. Don't be too hard on yourself, especially in the beginning. You have a lot to learn and absorb. There is a reason I encouraged you early in this book to take your time as you act on the suggestions at the end of each key. Whether you feel you need to do all five or to simply choose one or two, be patient as you get these habits established so they will become part of a long-term healthy lifestyle, not just things you do for a few weeks or months. In each key, all five are important, but you don't have to do them all at once.

The biggest favor you can do yourself is not to set the bar too high at first. If you have unrealistic expectations, you will probably end up discouraged. People who try to fix everything in one week often give up. Remember, these changes are supposed to last a lifetime!

There is no need to push yourself to the limit of your capacity unless you are training for the Olympics. You will improve simply by doing the right things regularly. And the only way you are going to do them regularly is if you start slowly, building better health day by day. As one thing becomes a natural part of your life, then you can move on to the next thing and you won't feel overwhelmed and want to quit.

This new way of living may not seem easy at first. Any time we break old bad habits and make new ones that are good for us, it presents challenges. You will definitely have to resist the temptation to give up and be willing to press on during those times when your progress is not going as fast as you would like. I am saying you can make it as easy on yourself as possible.

It Doesn't Have to Be Difficult

You can do a number of things to make your new lifestyle a relatively painless adjustment. In fact, it pays to start thinking early about the context in which you will introduce your new habits. For example, if you are going to start walking a mile a day, when are you going to do it? Try to pick a time when you will not feel pressure from some other aspect of your life. Where are you going to do it? Are you going to do it by yourself or with someone else? Arranging your life so your new healthy habits fit right in is a key to long-term commitment.

Let me ask you a few questions to get you thinking in the right direction. How can you introduce positive reinforcement into your plan? In what ways can you remove the temptation to fail? Are there people you can team up with who can help support your goals? Should you drop out of that dessert club you have belonged to for two years? Can you plan vacations that focus on health and fitness or on relaxation and spiritual refreshment?

If we get serious about it, there are innumerable ways most of us can tinker with our lives to help make success easier than failure. I know you can succeed. I believe you are on your way to great things and I am cheering you on.

Five Ways to Make Success Easy

1. Take Small Steps

Walking a mile takes about 2,000 steps. There are no other options or shortcuts. Every one of those steps is a tiny success that gets you closer to your goal. In the previous chapter, I wrote about the importance of setting your sights on your dreams and goals, and now I want to remind you how essential it is to break down those goals into doable steps.

If you concentrate only on your ultimate goals, it is easy to get lost halfway there. Plan your short-term goals so you have something within reach to aim for. Write them down so you can have a sense of whether or not you are on track. For example, if your ultimate goal is to walk three miles a day, five days a week, you might start off with only a half-mile three days a week. Do whatever you *think* you can do. The next week, you might aim for a mile on each of the three days, and so on, slowly upping your accomplishments without risking failure and disappointment. Be sure to embrace your little victories. Small successes breed large ones. Remember, you have nothing to prove to anyone but yourself. Reaching short-term realistic goals will encourage you to press on toward the big prize.

2. Laugh at Setbacks

No matter how carefully you plan your progress, you will have setbacks. That's part of life. One big difference between successful and unsuccessful people is not whether they have setbacks, or even the frequency of their setbacks, but how they respond to them. Successful people laugh off setbacks and get right back on track.

Having a bad day does not mean you have to have a bad life. You will have days when your program won't be as exciting as it seemed at first and days when you feel useless. That's fine. Don't be hard on yourself on such days. Be nurturing and supportive, as you would for anyone else you love. Remind yourself that 10 days forward and one day backward still ultimately gets you where you are going.

Consider writing down your victories as they happen. Keep a journal of your journey toward great health, inside and out, and record all your little successes. When you have a discouraging day or one where you feel you have done everything wrong, read your journal. You may be amazed at how far you have come.

3. Make It Convenient

If you are a busy person, you will have to find ways to fit the 12 keys into your schedule. Exercising takes time. Preparing or finding healthy foods takes time. Reading labels takes time. Praying takes time. Even reducing stress can take time. Fortunately, there are ways to make all these things convenient.

For example, don't think that to eat healthily you can never eat fast food again or must only eat at the local vegetarian restaurant. The major fast-food chains have been pressured into offering healthy foods, and some have gotten pretty good at it. Also, remember that exercise is convenient when it does not require you to drive anywhere, deal with special equipment, or otherwise burden your day. Choose an exercise program you can do. Don't make it something expensive that will take two hours out of your day. In addition, choose a hairstyle and clothing that make you feel good about yourself yet require little maintenance. You can look excellent and still be comfortable. As a final suggestion, choose where you live based on what will make your healthy lifestyle goals convenient, not on a prestigious neighborhood or a fantastic resale value. Can you take walks right out the front door? Are your church, school, and work easy, low-stress drives or grueling one-hour commutes? Do what is simple and you will enjoy your life more!

4. **Make It Fun**

You will only keep doing things if you enjoy them. God wants us to enjoy life to the fullest. Find an exercise you *like*. Find vegetables you *like*. Don't force down lima beans if you cannot stand the taste of them; it will only backfire. Exercise can be enjoyable if you focus on the long-term benefit instead of the immediate challenge. Obviously, you only get the spiritual and health benefits of church if you enjoy going. Shop around until you find one that resonates with your beliefs and style of worship—and you'll find that being part of a church can be really fun.

This point is worth thinking about carefully. Keep the concept of fun in the back of your mind the whole time you work toward a healthy lifestyle, because you are not getting healthy to make yourself miserable. I am not suggesting that we will never face a challenge or find the need to discipline ourselves in order to accomplish our goals, but we can make what we do as enjoyable as possible. The goal is to develop a life of spiritual and emotional joy, and that should be part of the payoff all along the way.

5. Reward Yourself

Don't underestimate the power of little rewards. Treating yourself to something that you enjoy after you reach your first short-term goal may give you something to look forward to. There is nothing wrong with making yourself feel good. As the old saying goes, "The carrot works much better than the stick."

Motivate yourself with something you will really enjoy once you reach a certain goal.

When you set short-term and long-term goals, go ahead and jot down some reasonable rewards with each one. Make sure the rewards are appropriate— big rewards for meeting your main goals and smaller tokens for your daily achievements or positive reinforcements. Just the knowledge that you are successfully reaching your goals may be enough motivation for you, but if not, use something to entice yourself.

Celebration can also be a big part of reaching your goals. Celebrations help give structure to your journey and let you reflect on what you have accomplished.

Act on It

Which of the five actions in this key will you take so you can make your journey

toward better health and a better life easier?
Write them below, commit to them, and start
today.

_____

_____

_____

KEY
12

Take Responsibility

One of the biggest problems in society today is that many people do not want to take responsibility for their lives. They want quick fixes. In many ways, our culture has trained people to believe that if they have problems, someone else is responsible. Their parents are responsible. Their spouses are responsible. Their schools or employers are responsible. The company that made the cigarettes or vehicle or junk food is responsible.

I think this passive mentality is dangerous. Maybe some people's parents did feed them a lot of junk food when they were young or never encouraged them to exercise. Maybe a person does have a genetic predisposition to store fat more than the average individual.

Maybe some people do have 60-hour-a-week jobs with long commutes that allow little time to prepare home-cooked meals. If any of these kinds of things apply to your life, the key to victory is to make the best you can out of them.

I am not saying you are completely responsible for the current state of your life. Lots of uncontrollable things happen to people. Sometimes we do get very bad training in childhood. Sometimes we have bad people in our lives and they hurt us. The circumstances in which you find yourself may or may not be your fault. But if you take these things lying down and do not try to make the best of them or rise above them, that *is* your fault. You do *not* have to stay in a bad situation. You get to make a choice, and that choice is 100% yours.

No matter how you got to the situation in which you find yourself today, don't let it be an excuse to stay there. I had many excuses and reasons for my poor health, bad attitude, and unbalanced life. As long as I made excuses, I never made progress. If you want to make progress and move beyond your current reality, believe you can do it and start taking action.

Taking responsibility for where we are is a must in making progress. Shifting blame keeps us trapped. It may put off a little guilt in the short term, but in the long run it just prolongs our misery. Determine today that you will take responsibility for your life and for the choices you make from now on. That's the best way to bring about the necessary changes and improvements you need in your life.

The Power of Free Will

Life would be so much easier if God had not given us free will. We could wander through our days like robots, eating the fruit that falls into our hands and waiting for the next thing to happen to us. But God does give us free will, which offers both tremendous responsibility and the possibility of total joy and fulfillment.

God will give you all the tools you need on Earth to reach spiritual completion. But it's up to you to take up those tools and put them to work restoring your health and renovating His temple (your body) for Him. He can make it as easy on you as possible—and in writing this book I have tried to help by giving you some useful information, guidance, and tips—but He can't do the work for you. The work is an essential part of the fulfillment, a necessary part of the process of freeing your soul from bondage. When you are in the depths of self-pity, free will can feel awful, like a pressure and responsibility you just don't want. But once you make the commitment to maintain your body and soul as you should, to be a person of excellence and power, you discover that free will is your most valuable possession.

This is why it is so important to take responsibility for your life and avoid self-pity at all costs. Self-pity is an emotion that feeds on itself and steals your power. You need power to become the person you are meant to be, and you cannot be pitiful and powerful at the same time. I had a major problem with self-pity in my earlier years, and I did not start making progress until I stopped feeling sorry for myself.

We feel better about ourselves when we approach life boldly, ready to be accountable and responsible. You don't have to hide from anything. You can do whatever you need to do in life. You can look healthy and attractive. You can feel great inside and out. You can live a life that keeps you fit and happy into old age. It's all up to you. Through God you are ready for anything. Confront your life head on and never turn back!

One Way to Take Responsibility for Your Life

Thus far I have suggested five options for implementing each of the 12 keys to good health and full enjoyment of your life. In this chapter, I'm not going to offer five ways. When it comes to taking responsibility for your own life, there is only one way to do it. The time has come to be very honest with yourself and with God. You either do it or you don't. Using everything you have learned in this book, you can easily break your old habits and begin the process of transforming your life. Make the decision to do so. When you have a moment of privacy, take a deep breath, clear your head, and repeat this phrase:

"I am responsible for my own life. No one can take charge of it but me. If I am unhappy or unhealthy, I know I have the power to change that. I have all the help and knowledge I need, and with God's help today I start becoming the person of excellence I have always known I can be."

Congratulations. Thanks for taking this journey with me, and blessings on you for the exciting and wonderful future that is just beginning for you.

Act on It

Choose to take responsibility for your life and for your health. Write your decision below, *commit to it*, and start today.

_____

_____

_____

YOUR KEYS TO GOOD HEALTH

Use this page to help yourself keep track of—and stick with—the 12 behaviors you have chosen to incorporate into your life for good health. On the lines provided below, write the behaviors or practices to which you committed yourself at the end of each key.

Key 1—Get God's Help:

_____

_____

_____

Key 2—Learn to Love Your Body:

_____

_____

_____

Key 3—Master Your Metabolism:

_____

_____

_____

Key 4—Exercise:

_____

_____

_____

Key 5—Eat in Balanced Ways:

_____

_____

_____

Key 6—Water Your Life:

_____

_____

_____

Key 7—Be Mindful About Eating:

_____

_____

_____

Key 8—Curb Your Spiritual Hunger:

_____

_____

_____

Key 9—De-Stress:

_____

_____

_____

Key 10—Live with the Right Vision:

_____

_____

_____

Key 11—Make It Easy:

_____

_____

_____

Key 12—Take Responsibility:

_____

_____

_____

DAILY CHECKLIST FOR GOOD HEALTH

You can invest in a good life and good health for your future by putting in a little time each day for personal upkeep, knowing you will get to "spend" all that time, plus interest, over the years of a long, healthy life. Use the checklist below to keep yourself on track each day. You can photocopy this list or create your own.

Daily Tasks

Nutrition

_____ Drink 6 to 10 glasses of water
_____ Eat 5 servings of fruits and vegetables
_____ Eat 2 servings of healthy protein (fish, poultry, eggs, beans, etc.)
_____ Take a multivitamin or supplement(s)

Hygiene

_____ Brush
_____ Floss
_____ Clean and moisturize skin
_____ Make hair and nails clean and attractive

Lifestyle

_____ Exercise: (name activity and duration)
_____ Dress in a way I feel good about
_____ Wear comfortable and supportive shoes
_____ Get a full night's sleep

Spirit

_____ Reduce or avoid stress (How?)
_____ Renew my spirit (How?)
_____ Do something for someone else (What?)
_____ Think about my long-term goals

General Reminders

- Protect your back when lifting.
- Avoid excessive sun exposure.
- Don't smoke.
- Preserve your eyes by not straining because of inadequate light or using incorrect glasses.
- Smile and laugh often.
- Don't do anything in excess.
- Get yearly checkups.
- Wash your hands frequently to avoid infections.
- Get six-month dental cleanings.
- Pray about everything throughout the day.
- Enjoy your life!

ABOUT THE AUTHOR

JOYCE MEYER is one of the world's leading practical Bible teachers. Her TV and radio broadcast, *Enjoying Everyday Life*, airs on hundreds of television networks and radio stations worldwide.

Joyce has written more than 100 inspirational books. Her bestsellers include *God Is Not Mad at You*; *Making Good Habits, Breaking Bad Habits*; *Do Yourself a Favor... Forgive*; *Living Beyond Your Feelings*; *Power Thoughts*; *Battlefield of the Mind*; *Look Great, Feel Great*; *The Confident Woman*; *I Dare You*; and *Never Give Up!*

Joyce travels extensively, holding conferences throughout the year, speaking to thousands around the world.

JOYCE MEYER MINISTRIES
U.S. & FOREIGN OFFICE ADDRESSES

Joyce Meyer Ministries
P.O. Box 655
Fenton, MO 63026
USA
(636) 349-0303

Joyce Meyer Ministries—Canada
P.O. Box 7700
Vancouver, BC V6B 4E2
Canada
(800) 868-1002

Joyce Meyer Ministries—Australia
Locked Bag 77
Mansfield Delivery Centre
Queensland 4122
Australia
(07) 3349 1200

Joyce Meyer Ministries—England
P.O. Box 1549
Windsor SL4 1GT
United Kingdom
01753 831102

OTHER BOOKS BY JOYCE

The Power of Simple Prayer
The Love Revolution*
The Secret Power of Speaking God's Word
The Secret to True Happiness

DEVOTIONALS

Battlefield of the Mind Devotional
The Confident Woman Devotional
Ending Your Day Right*
Hearing from God Each Morning
Love Out Loud
New Day, New You
Power Thoughts Devotional
Starting Your Day Right*
Trusting God Day By Day

* Also available in Spanish